Once Upon A Time…
The Guide To FREE Self-publishing"

← → C 🔒 https://tsw.createspace.com/title/5778190/covercreator/paperback?serviceId=39411021&taskKey=cover_creator_form&designID=0&taskID=59073017&ac ☆ ≡

Tasks	7 of 9 tasks completed

► Author(s) 🟢

▼ Front Cover Image 🟢

☑ Visible

Alignment And Rotation:

Image : Love____a_Dove_Cover_for_Kindle.jpg

Use one of our images	Upload	Clear

Instructions:

Please upload an image (jpeg or tiff) at the size of 5.5" x 4.75" (width and height) and with an image resolution of at least 300 DPI. Please note that images uploaded at a different size will be proportionately sized to fit.

If you submit an image that contains text, please make sure all text is at least 0.5" from the outer edges.

If you wish to use the default image, uncheck the "Visible" box above.

Next

Current Design: The Poplar 8.5 x 8.5 Spineless

Change Design

100%	200%	Hide Frames	Show Rulers

THE GUIDE TO FREE
SELF-PUBLISHING

Love..........
a Dove

by Bradley Zink

BY BRADLEY ZINK

Barcode Area

Made with Cover Creator

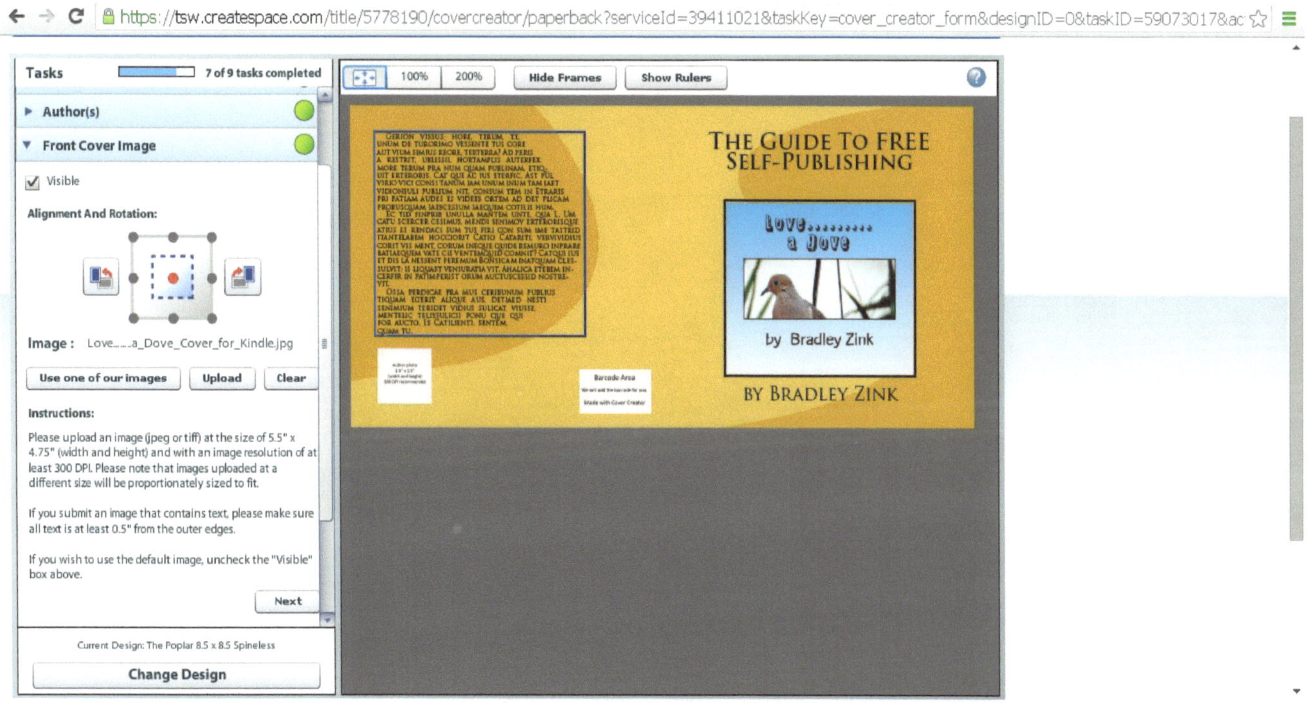

by

Bradley Zink

ISBN: 1517641713
ISBN-13: 978-1517641719

DEDICATION

This book is dedicated to ALL authors, both published and inspiring. To have the vision, and transcribe it into a book is a true artform.

Writers always write, and this book is to help those who want to get their visions published.

ACKNOWLEDGMENTS

I would like to thank Anthony A LoBue "Tony the Vet", for inspiring me 'create' this step-by-step book on how to self-publish your book.

This book stems from the concept of a class for Veterans, active duty and their spouses I taught at the Veterans Museum in Balboa Park. The hopes of the class is to show an "outlet" for our military personnel to express themselves. With the mental strain that their careers carry, many suffer mentally.

This book, and the series of classes I'm teaching, is a way to show them that they can 'control' some aspect in life, through 'Art'.

God Bless Our Troops!

This book is to serve as a simple step-by-step guide to self-publishing for free online. There are many different companies that offer to self-publish your books for free, and there are a lot of good companies. I chose to use Createspace, and am therefore using their website as the guide to self-publishing. I do not work for, nor am endorsing this company over others; simply use this company for it ease of use, simple setup process, and visibility online.

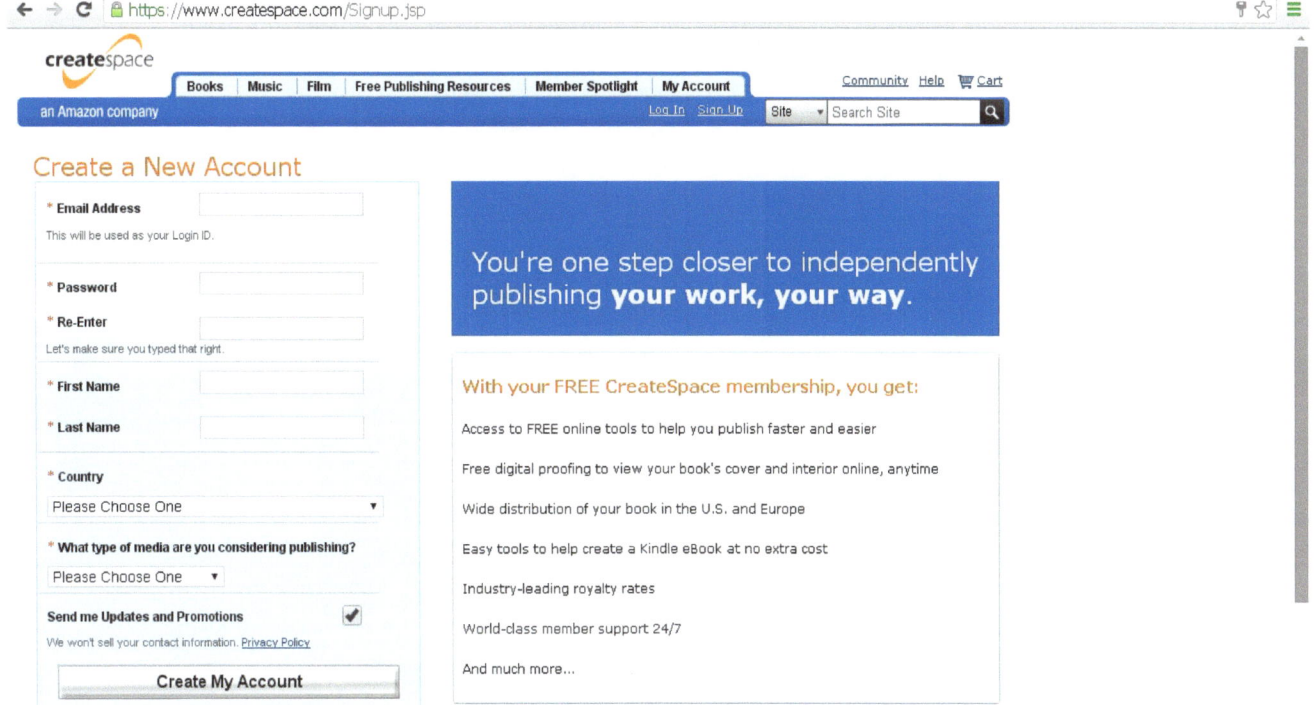

Account Setup Screen

Fill in the information requested and create a login and password. This process takes just minutes to complete, then you're ready to start publishing!

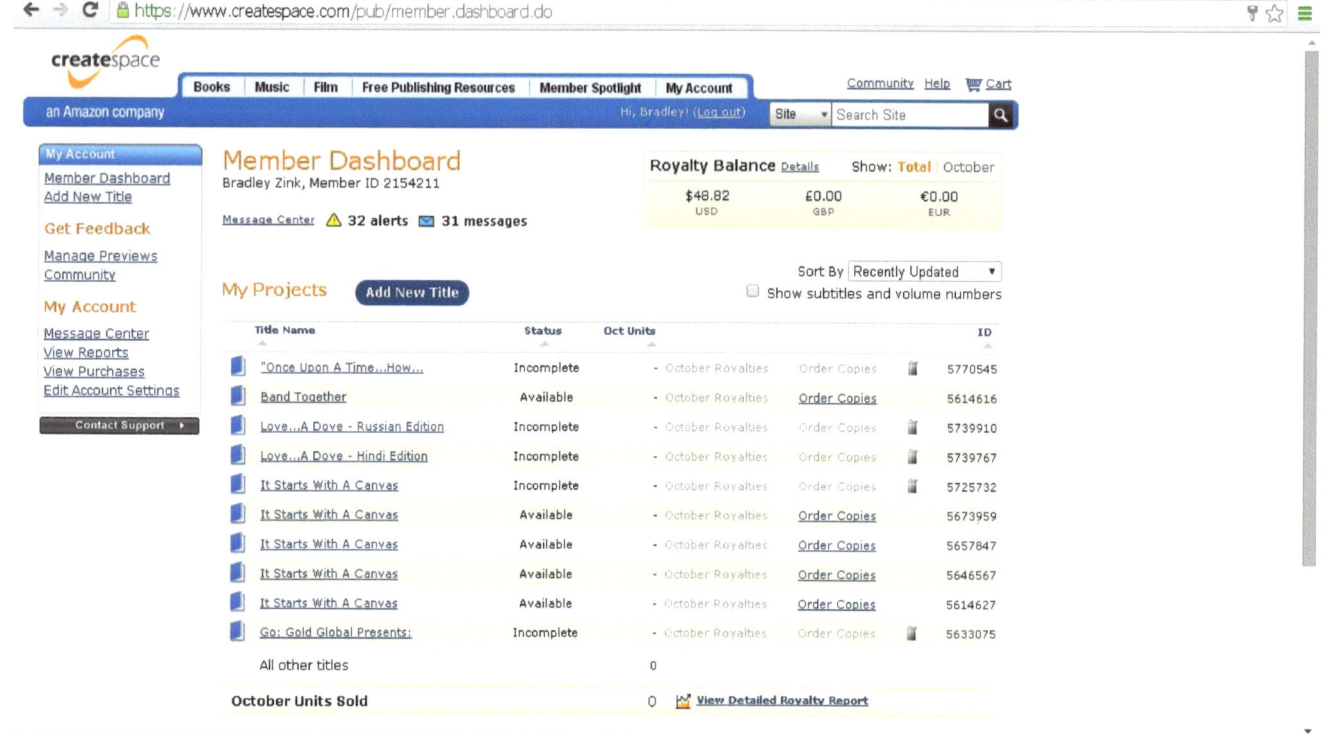

Member Dashboard

This will be the Main screen for your account. Here you can Add a new title, see current projects, message and alert notices, as well as your Royalty Balance.

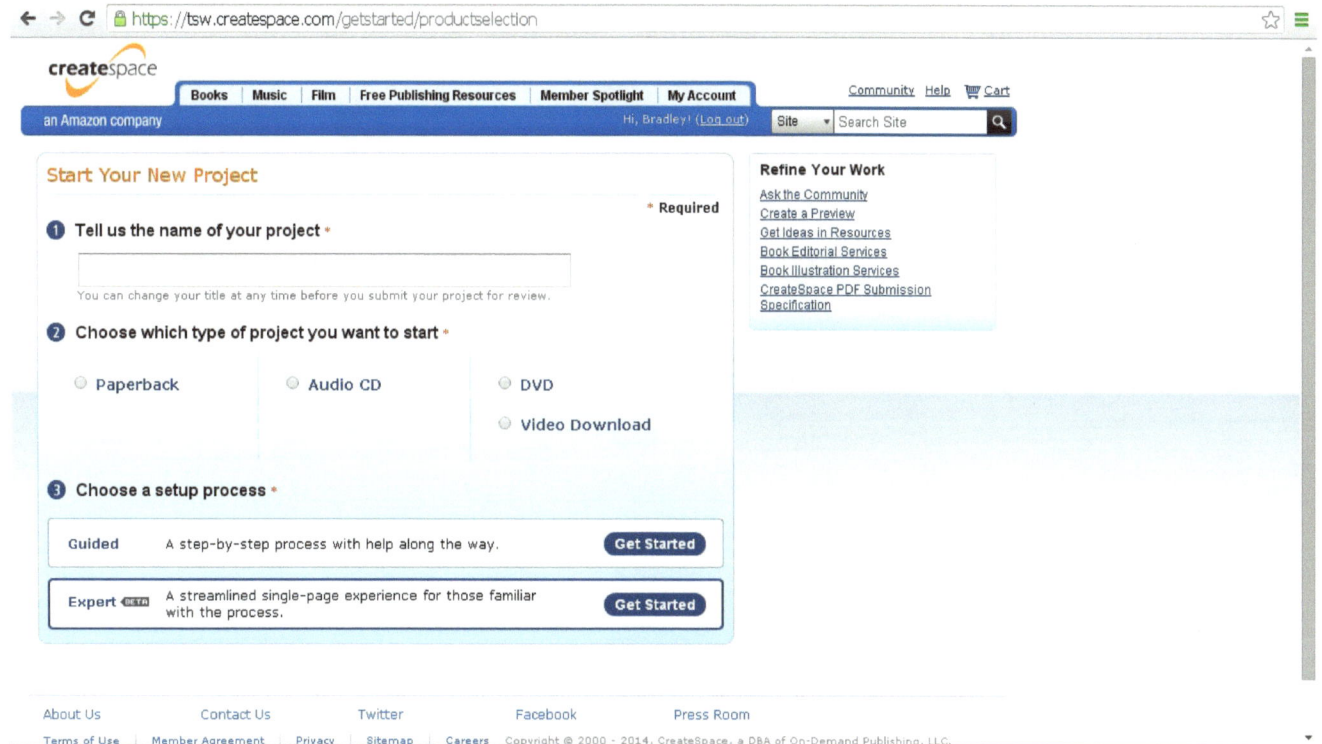

Start New Project

Once you have clicked Add New Title, you are taken to the Start New Project Screen. Here you will Enter the Title of your project, choose the type of project you are creating, as well as selecting your Setup Process. Select Guided for the first project you work on, for an more user-friendly process.

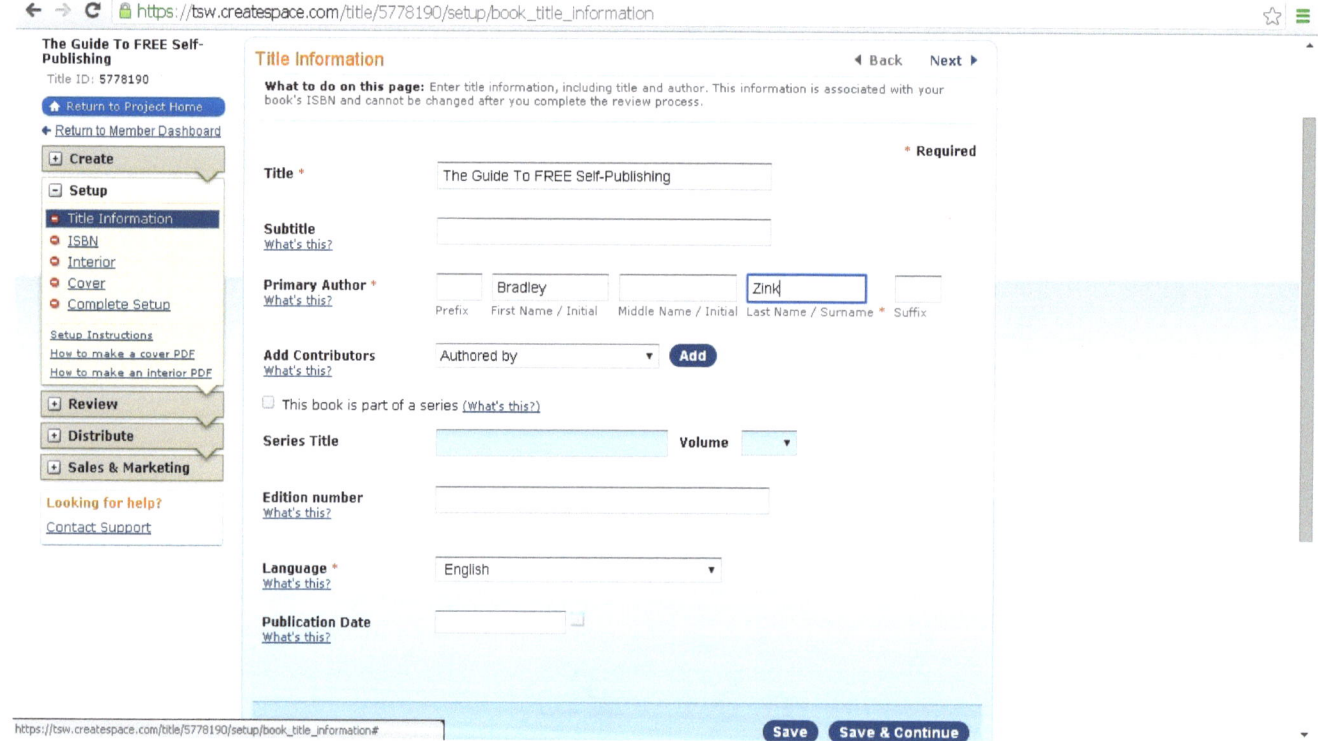

Title Setup

At the Title Information screen, you will verify Title of your project, add subtitle (if applicable), author's name and other contributors (if applicable), as well as language project will be in.

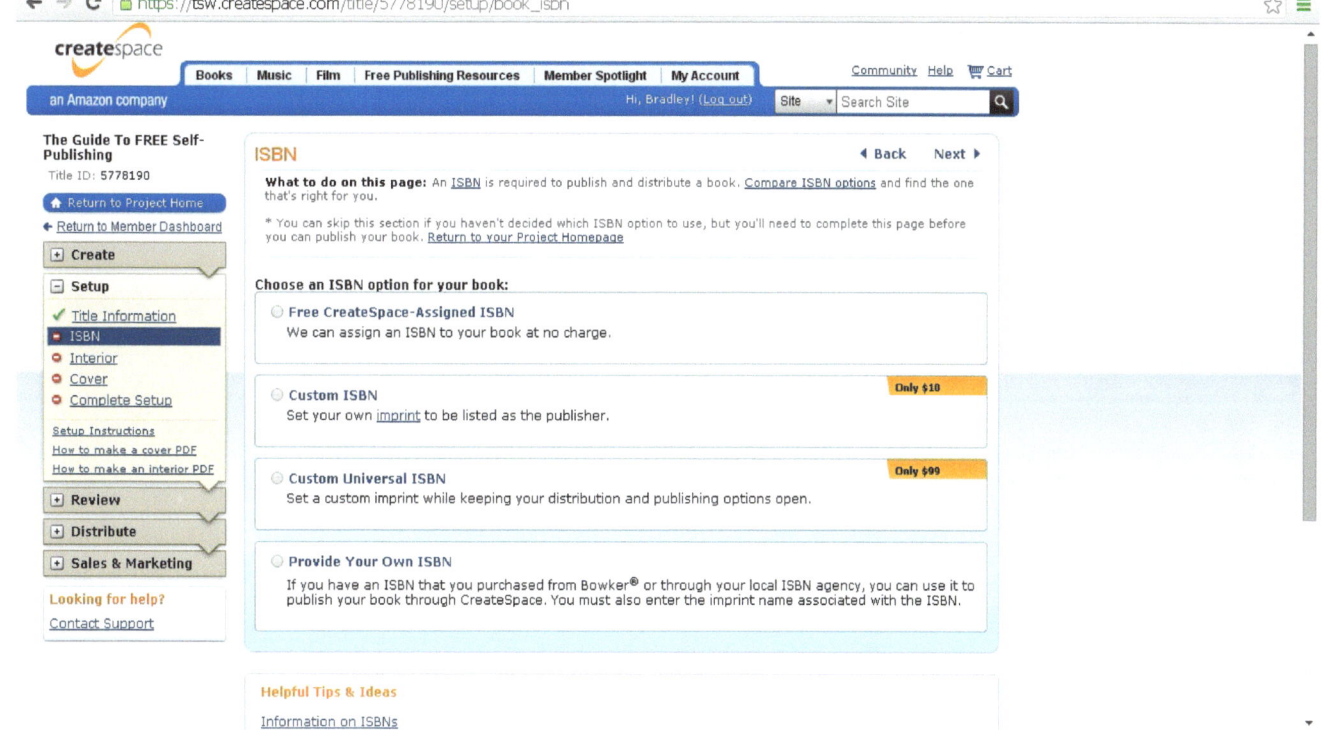

ISBN Setup

Next you will choose your ISBN option. There are options for a Free ISBN, Custom, Custom Universal and Provide Your Own (if purchased prior).

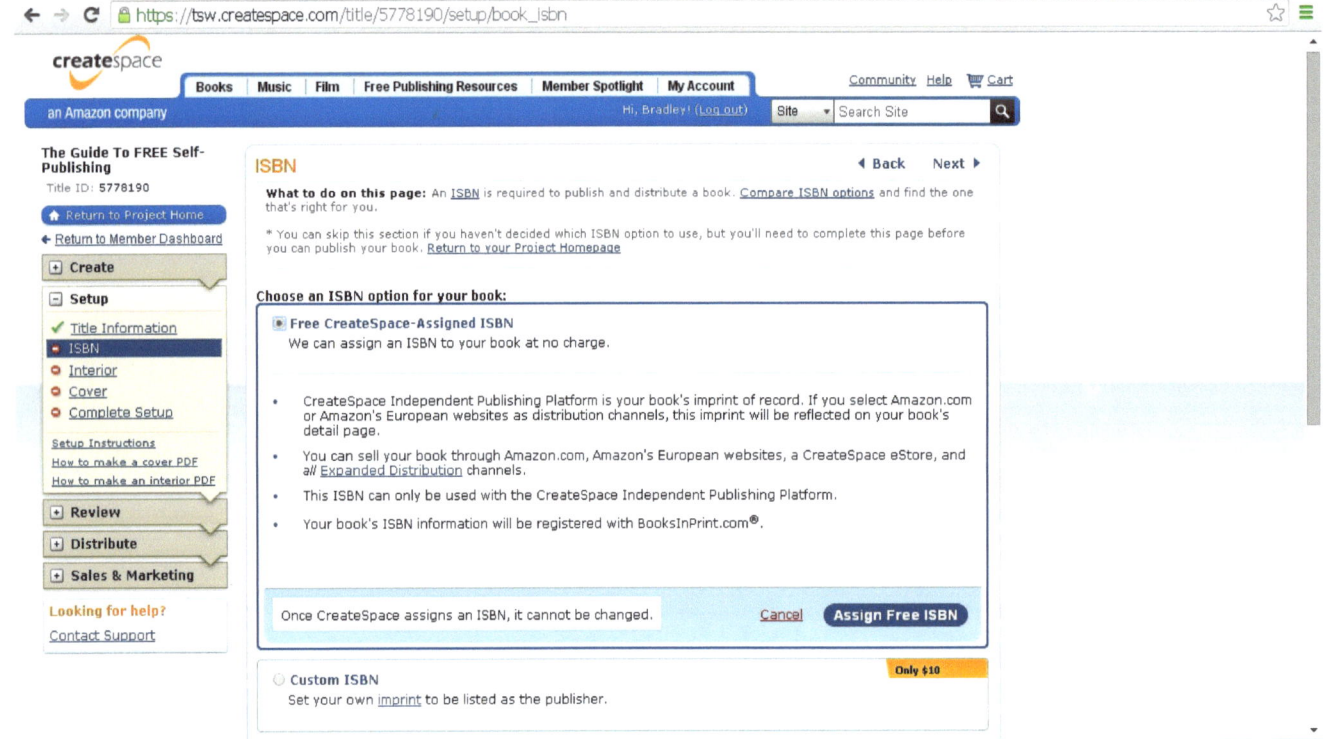

Free ISBN Option

To truly make this a Free publishing process, simply select Free Createspace assigned ISBN. Be sure to read each option, and choose which best fits your needs.

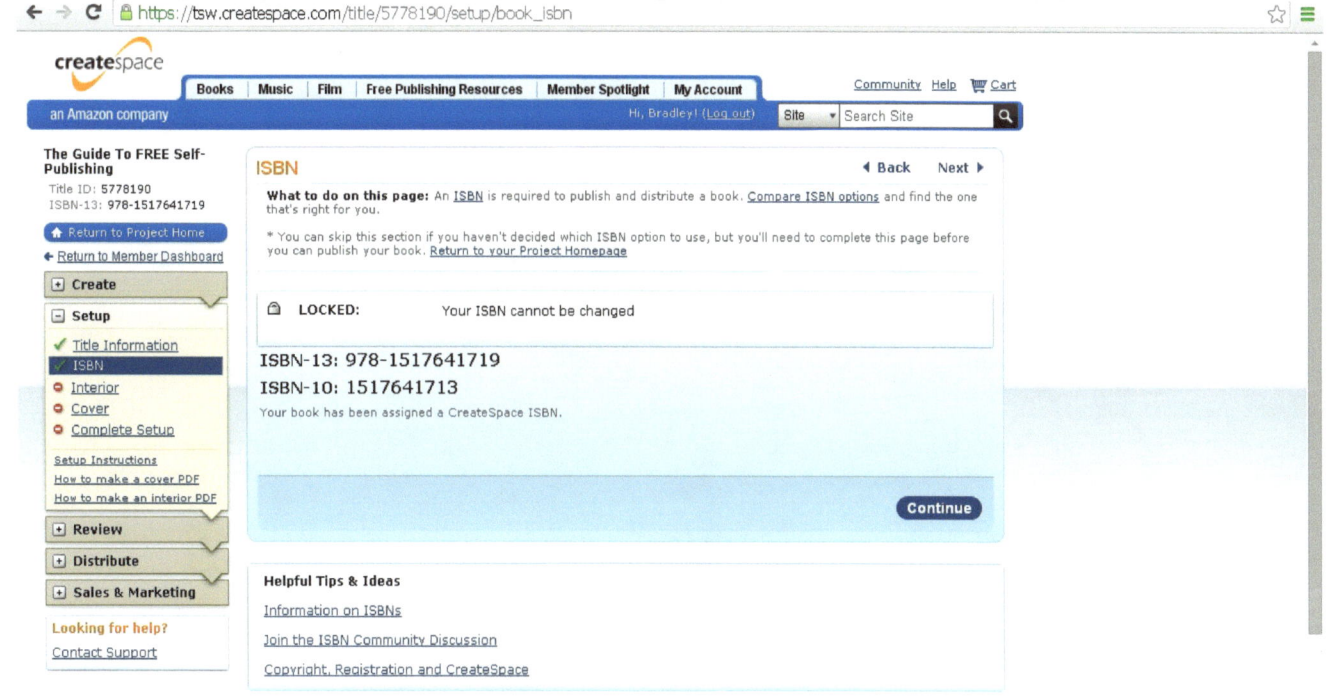

ISBN Assigned

Your ISBN is now assigned and locked. This number cannot be changes, and will be registered with the Library of Congress linked to your title. Make note of these (2) ISBN numbers, both ISBN-10 and ISBN-13. You will need to put these in the interior of your book.

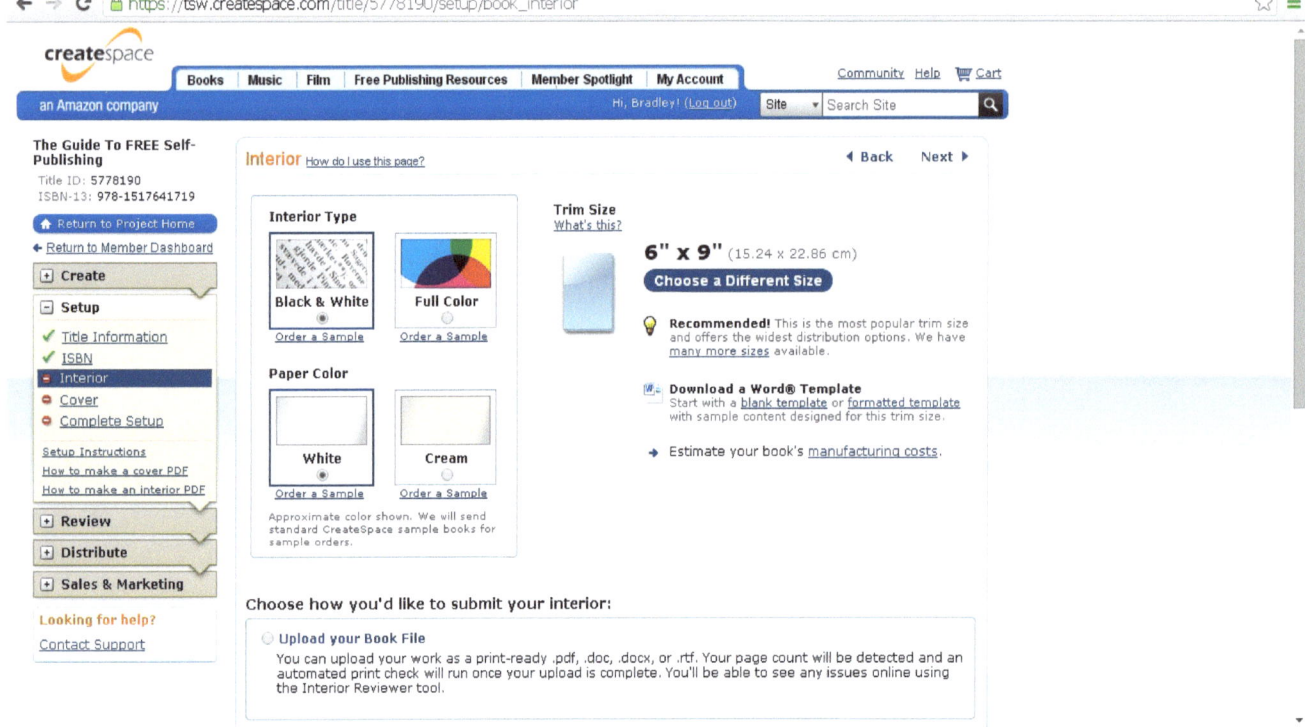

Interior Setup

The Interior Setup section is where you can choose the main options for your type of book. Select the option of either Black & White or Color (make note that color books cost slightly higher to print). Select the type of paper color, White or Cream (some size options only print on white). Also, you will choose the size for your book, or Trim Size. Click on Choose a Different Size to see several selection options.

Trim Size Selection

A few examples of different Trim Size options. Click the one you prefer to continue. Once back at the Interior Screen, you can Download a Word Template of your Trim Size. You can select either Blank or Formatted (includes Cover page, Title of Contents page, as well as several Chapter pages already formatted).

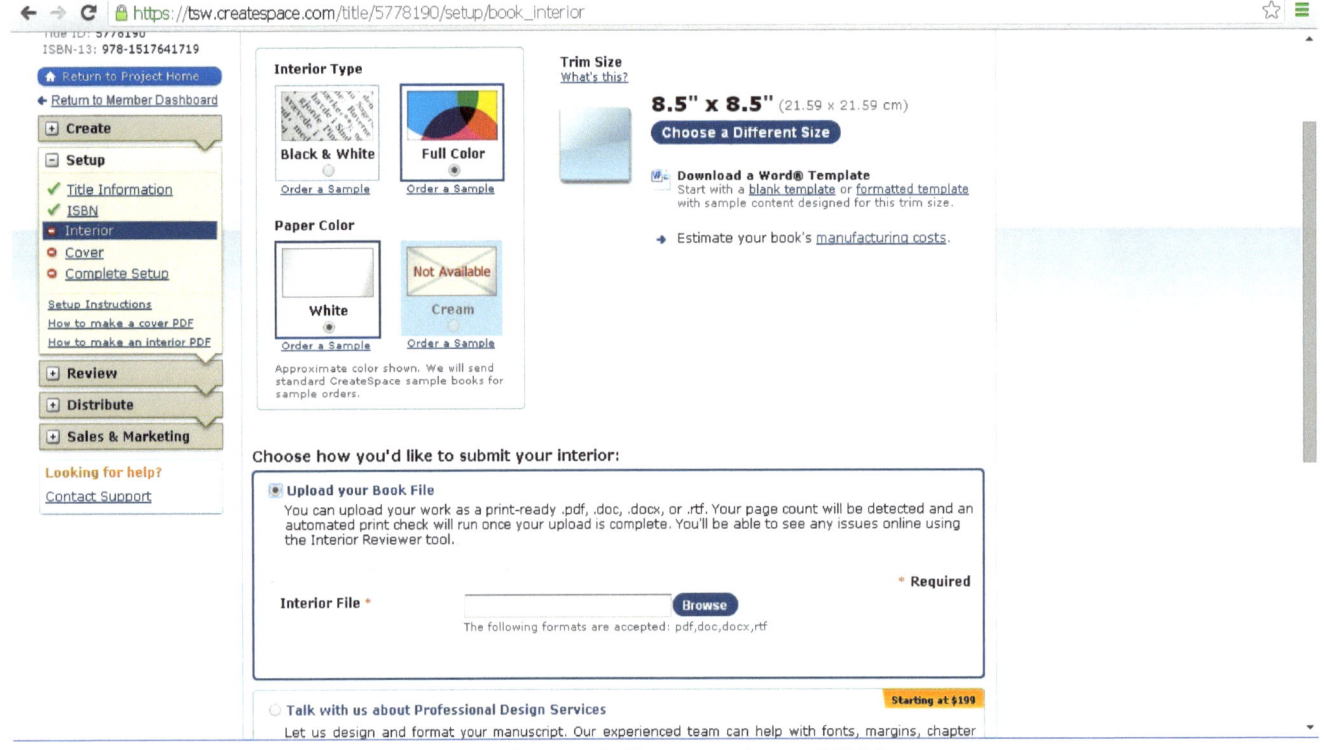

Upload Interior File

After you have completed your book in Word, simply upload the file to continue the process.

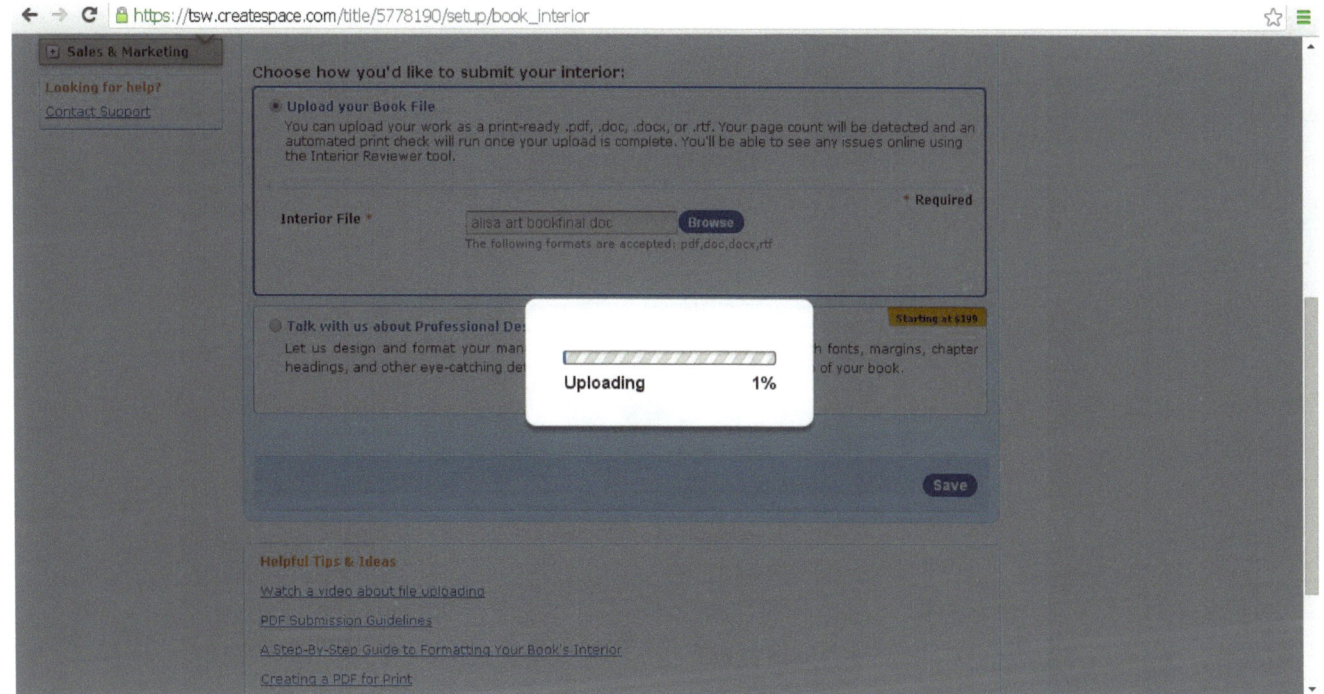

Interior Upload

Your book will be uploaded to Createspace's website, and automatically converted to PDF format.

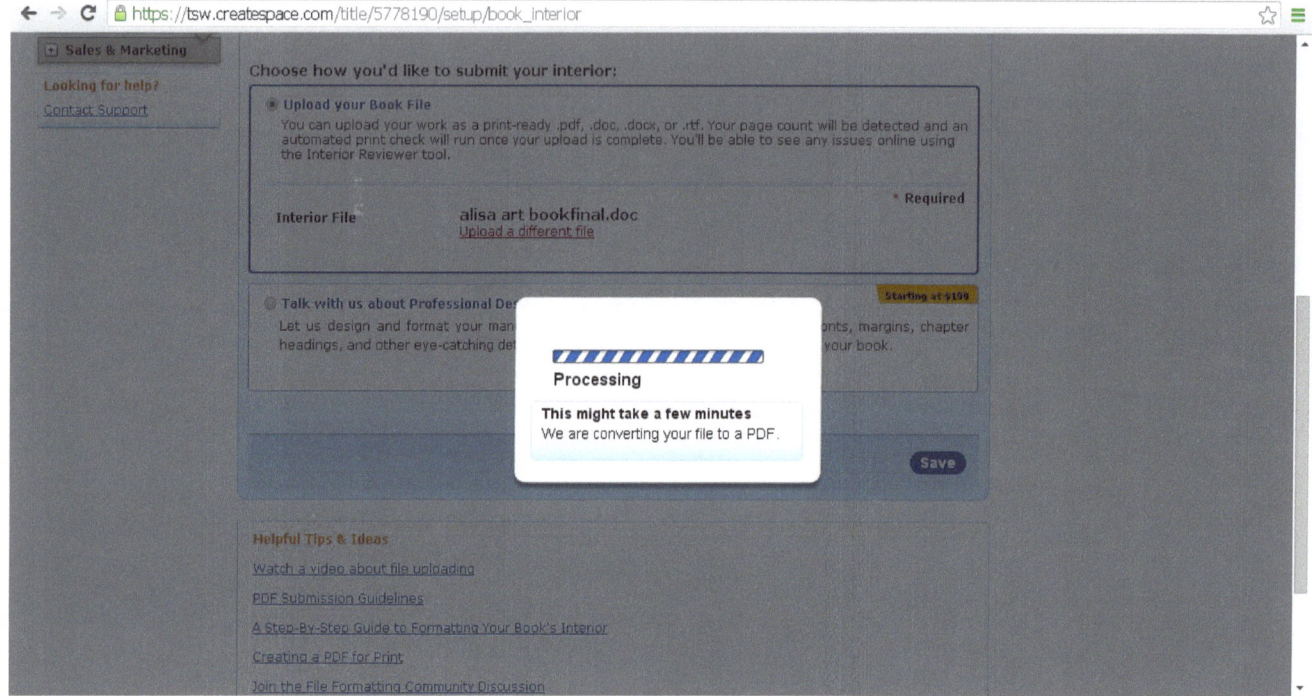

Interior Upload PDF Conversion

The conversion process can take several minutes to complete, depending on size and length of your book.

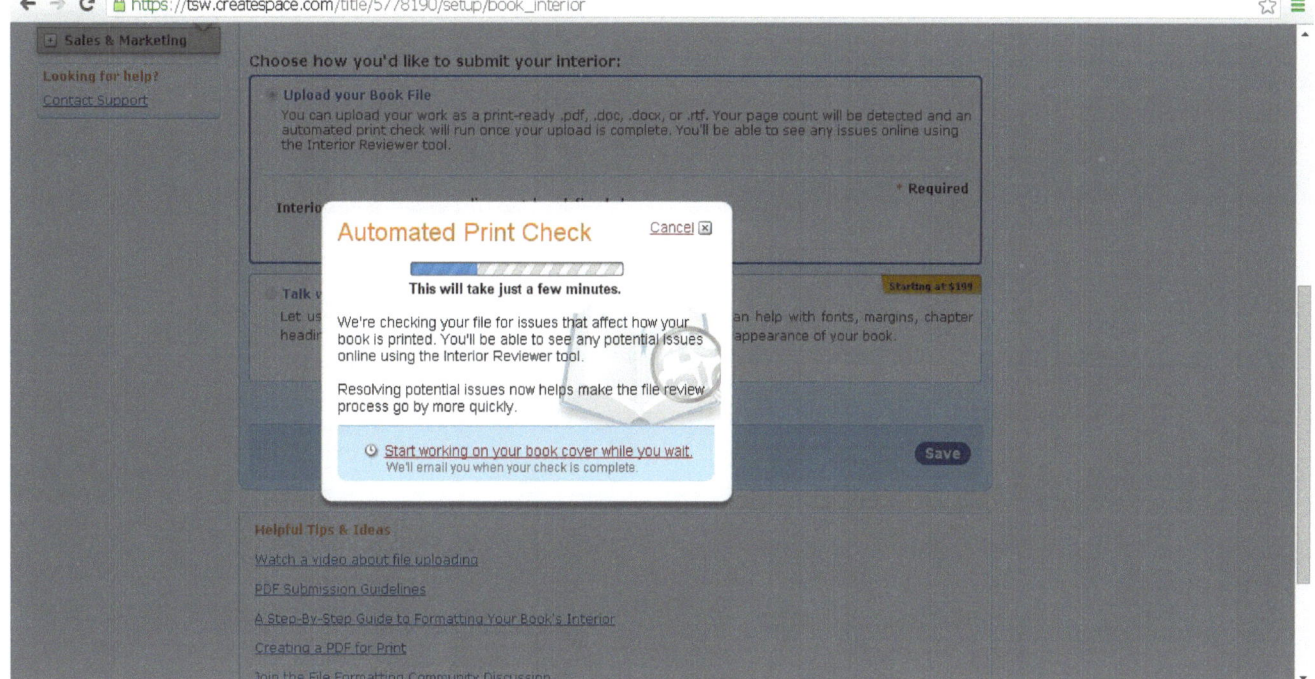

Automated Print Check

After file is uploaded and converted, Createspace will run a simple Automated Print Check of your file, to see if it meets the standards set for printing. While this can take several minutes as well, you can Start working on your book cover while you wait.

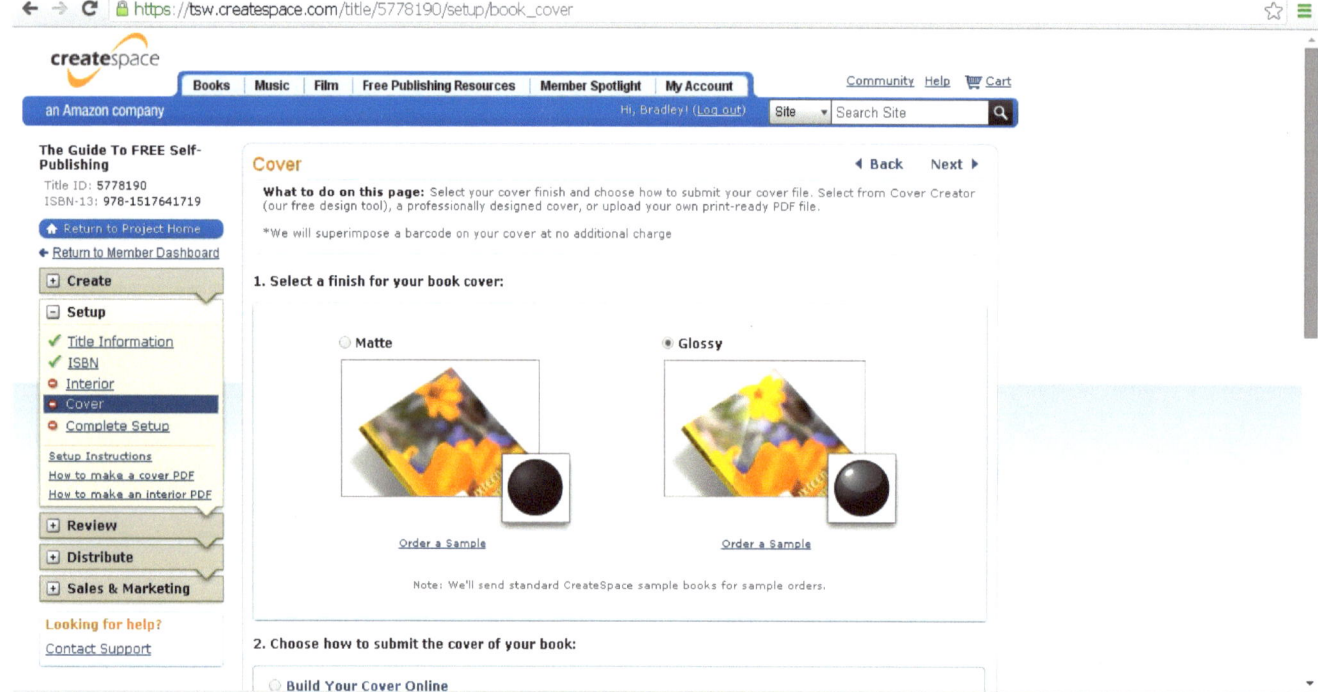

Cover Setup

At the Cover setup screen, you will select which type of cover you'd like for your book, Matte (a flat-like finish) or Glossy (a high-gloss shine).

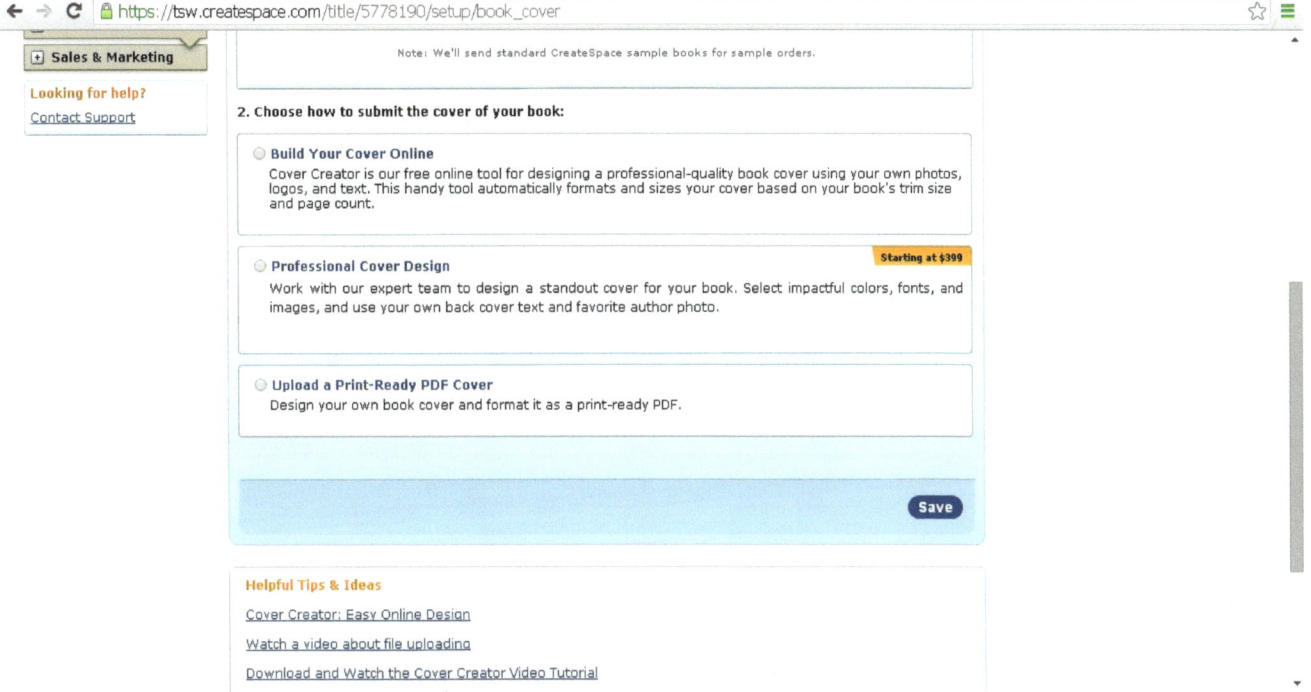

Cover Setup Options

Next, you will select how to submit a cover. There are 3 options to choose from: Build Your Cover Online (free step-by-step service), Professional Cover Design (for a fee), or Upload a Print-Ready PDF Cover (if you've already designed one).

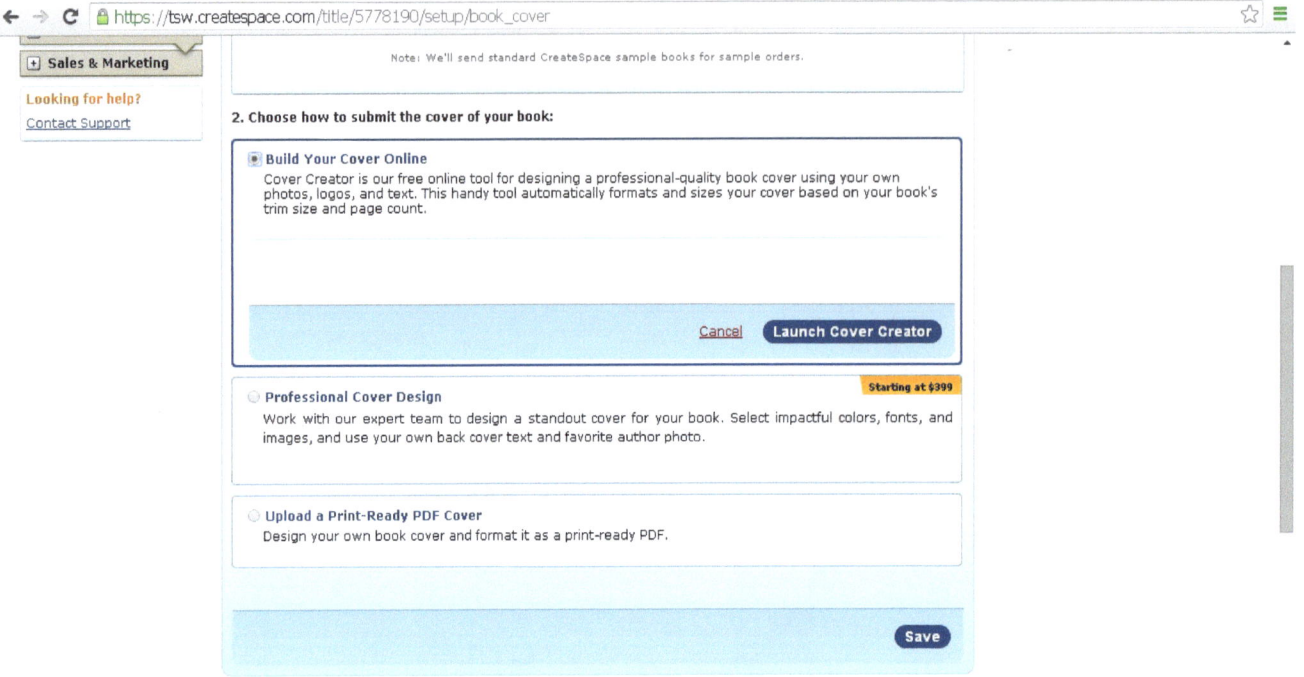

Build Cover Online

To keep this entire process Free, select Build Your Cover Online, then click Launch Cover Creator.

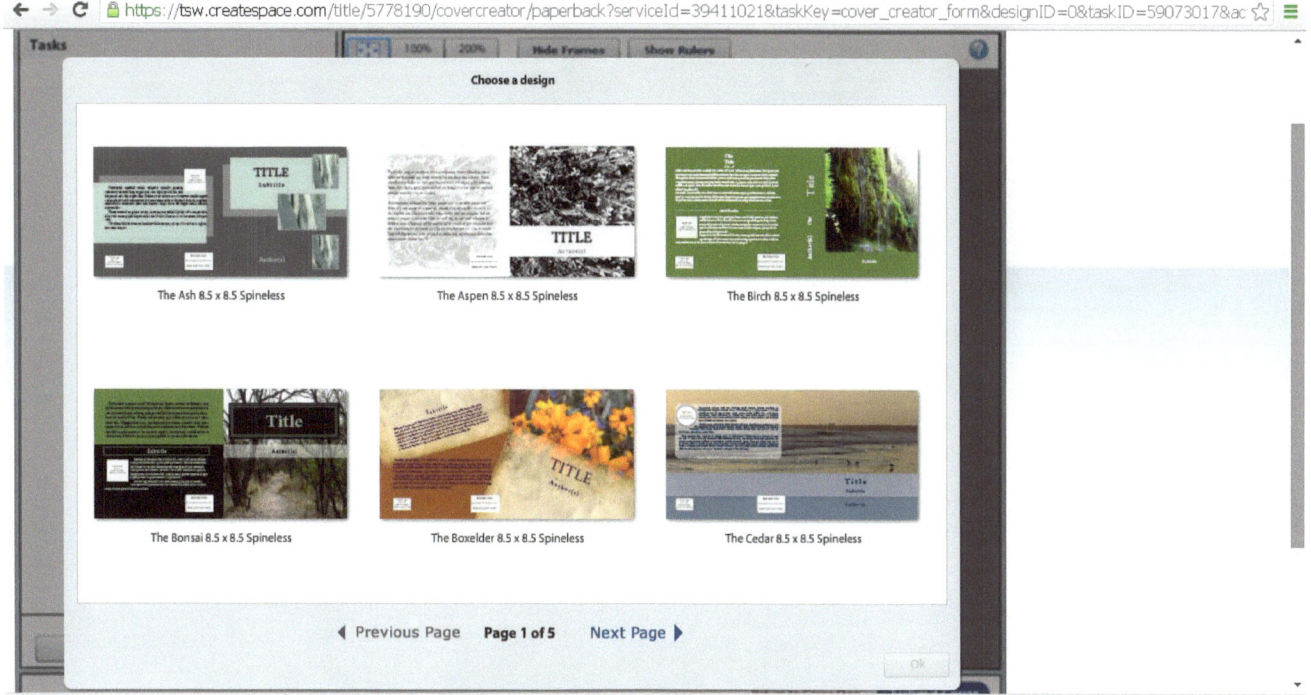

Cover Design

Once the Cover Creator launches, you will first need to select a Cover Design. There are several different styles to choose from.

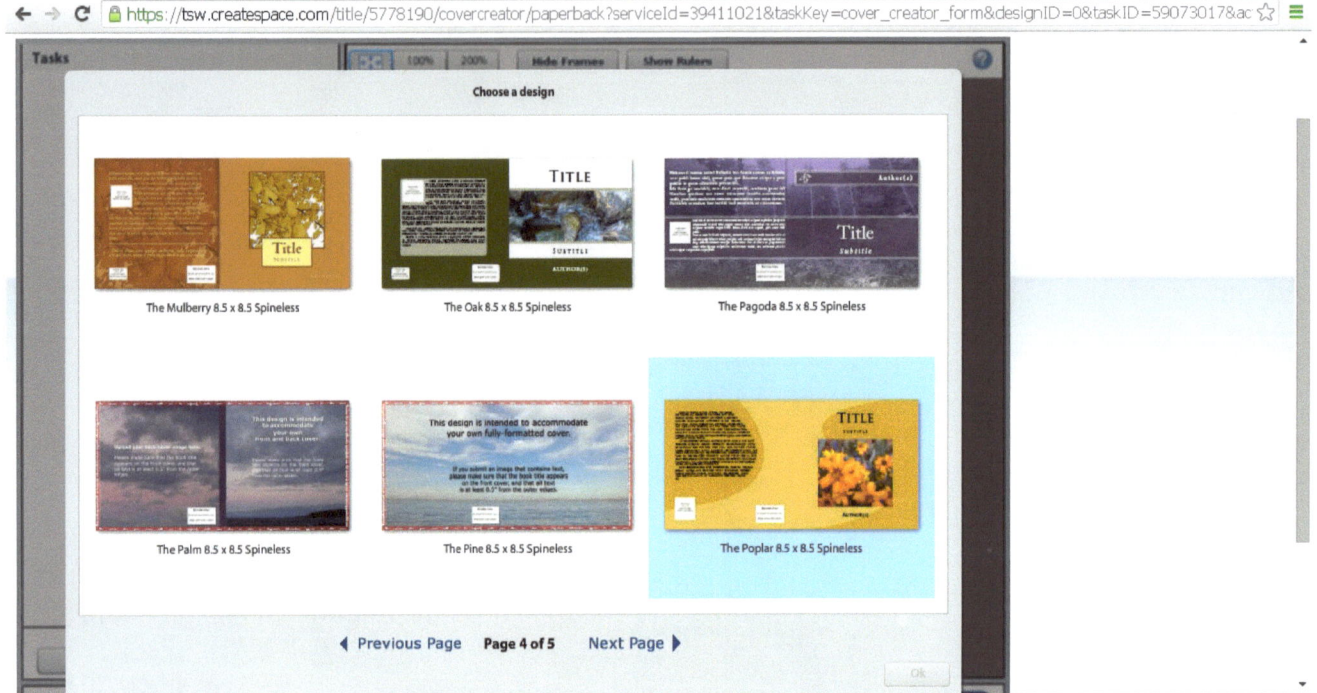

Cover Design Select

Once you have found the cover you like, simply click on it to select and continue. Next you will be taken to the complete design section.

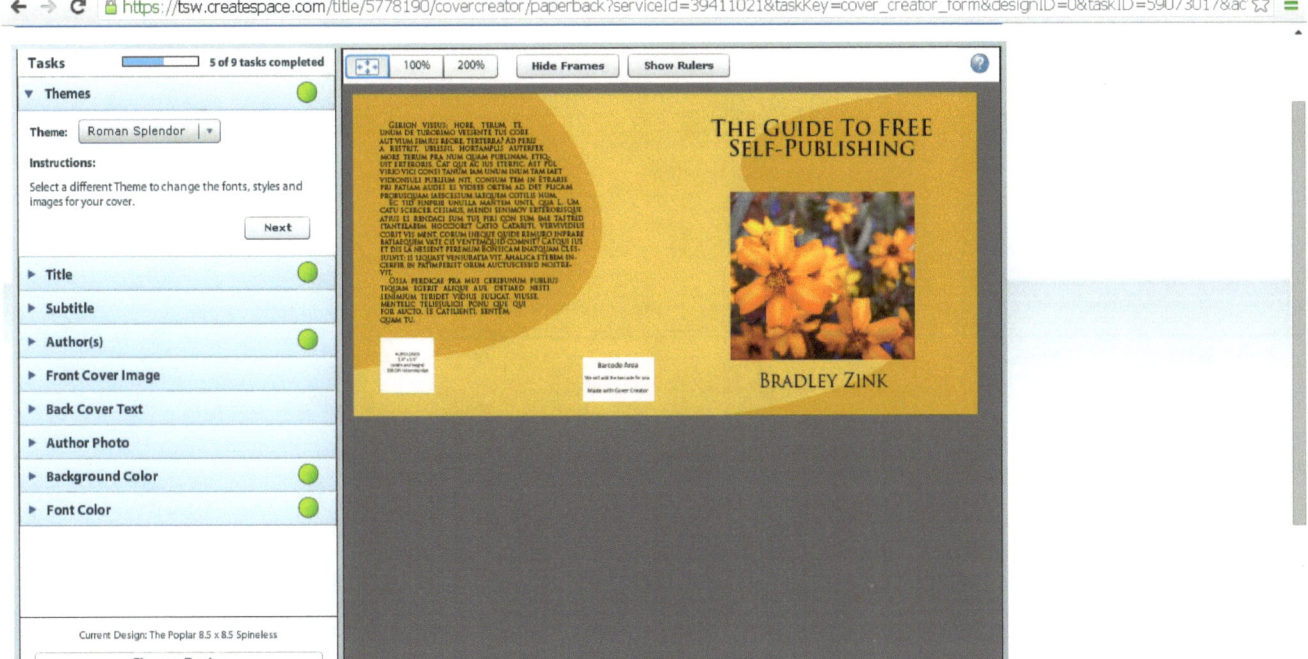

Cover Design Tasks

Cover Design Tasks are the different sections of your cover that you will create. The tasks vary, depending on the Cover Design you selected on the previous screen.

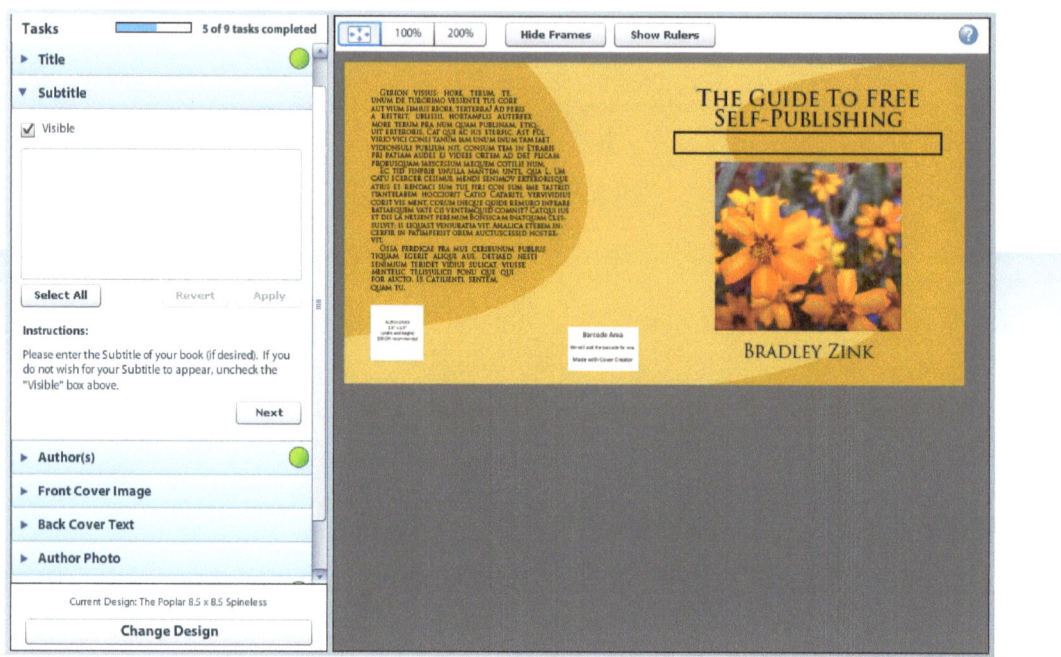

Cover Design Visible

As you will notice, some tasks have already been completed automatically, like the Title and Author. These were auto-filled from information you entered earlier. Some tasks can either be visible or not on your cover, depending on your preferences. If you do not have a subtitle for your book, simply uncheck the Visible box, click apply and the item will be removed.

Cover Design Apply

When you click the Apply button, you will see this little 'thinking' pattern display as task is being completed. Click Next to go to the Front Cover Image task.

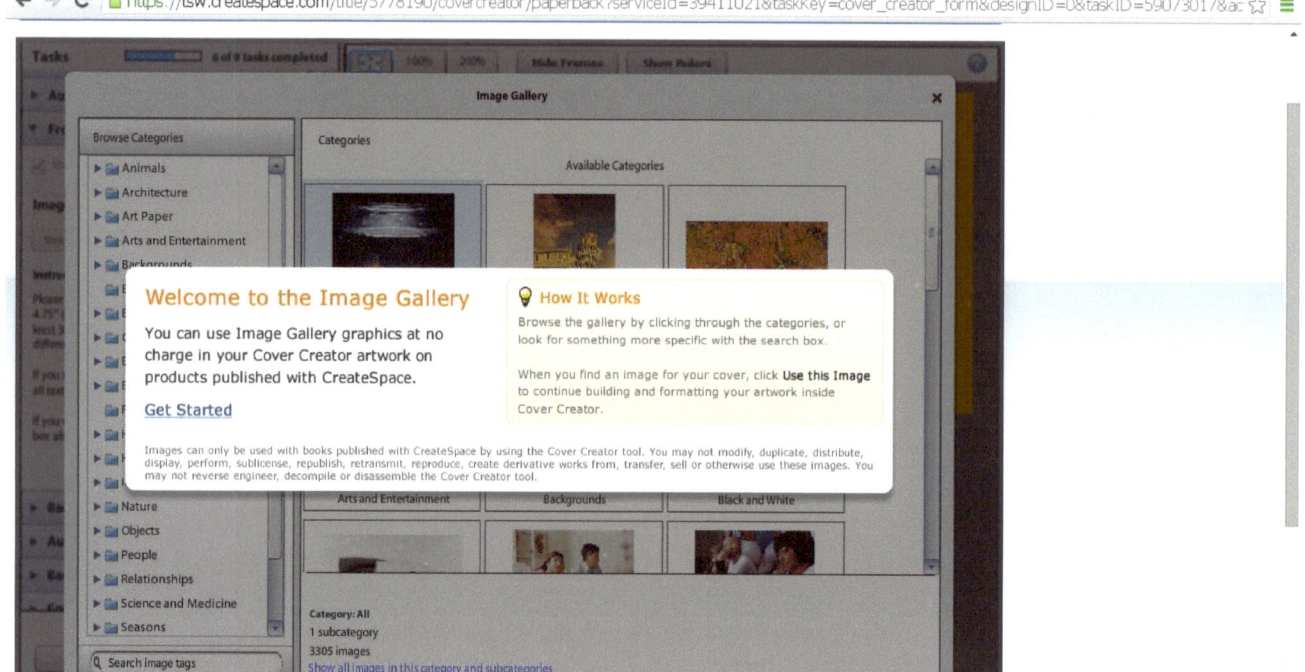

Cover Image Gallery

For your cover image, you can use a picture of your own, or choose from Createspace's Image Gallery. Here you will find several themes and images to choose from.

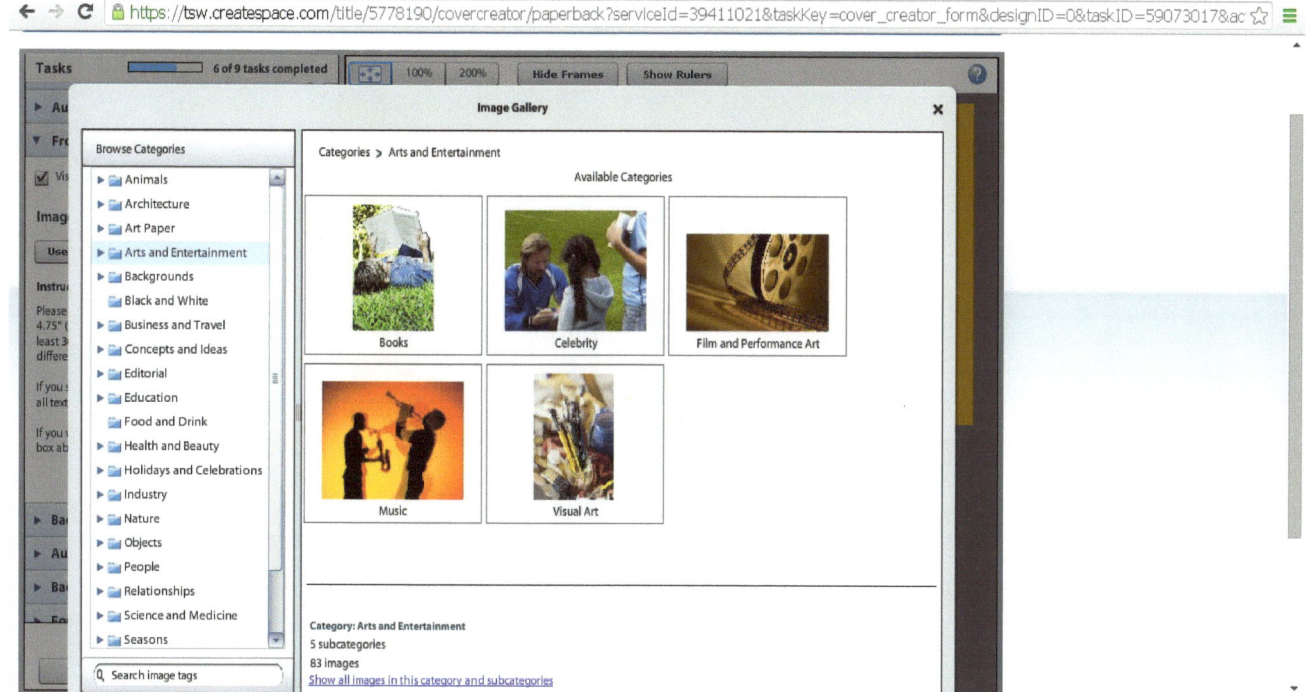

Cover Image Subcategory

Several Categories have subcategories for a wide range of images to choose from.

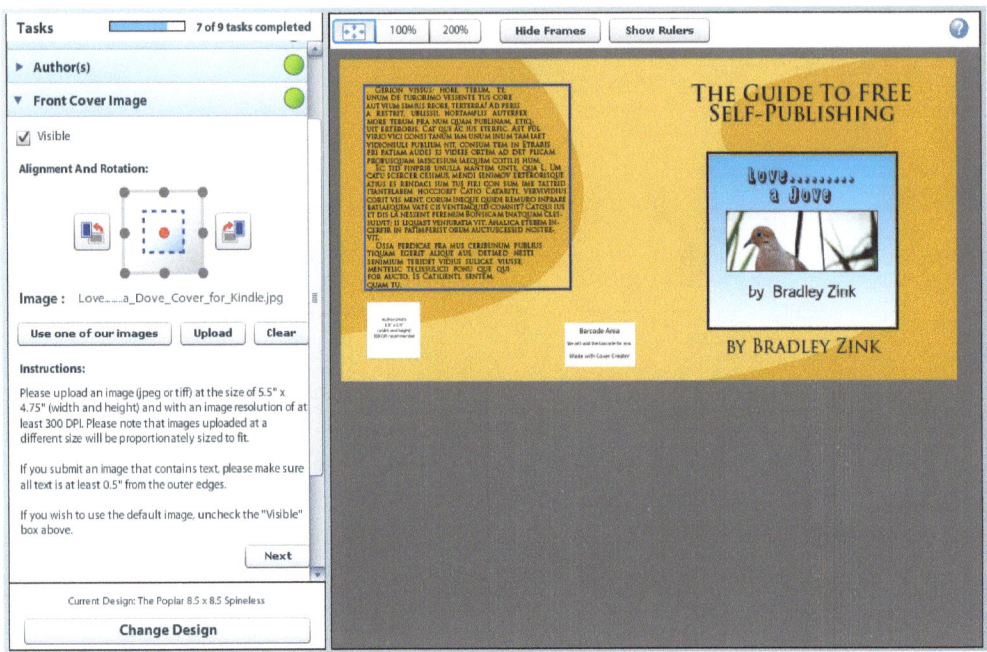

Cover Image Align

Once you've either uploaded or chosen an image from the Image Gallery, you can align the image on the cover.

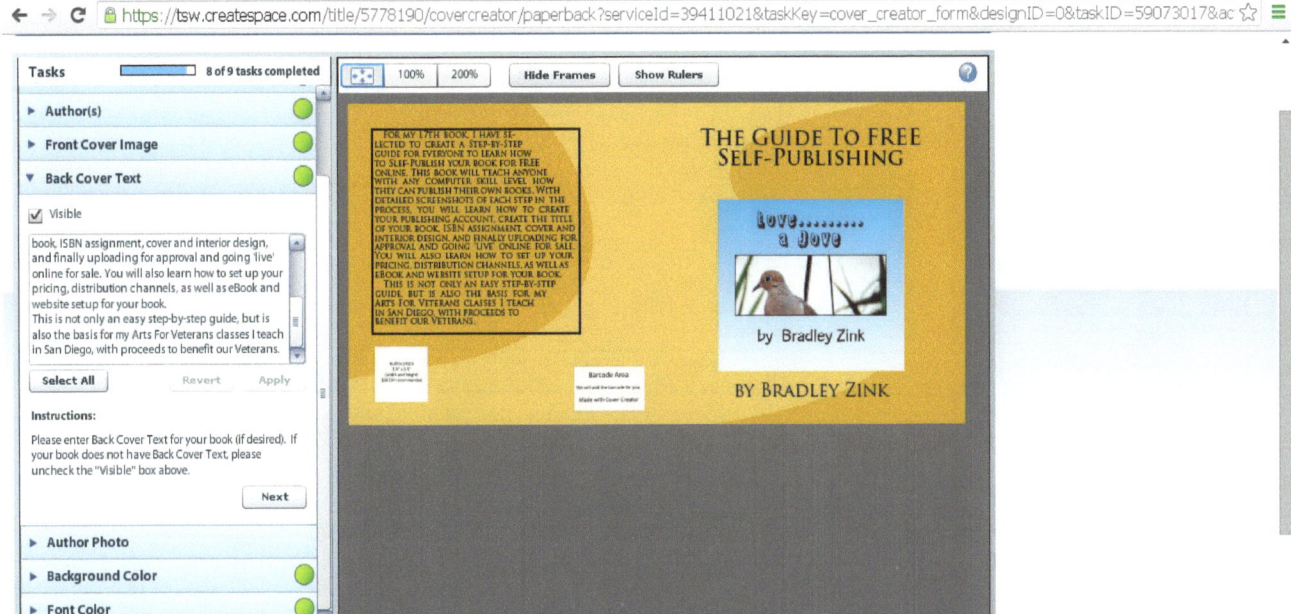

Back Cover Text

The Back Cover Text is the place where you can tell people a brief synopsis about the book, or any other information you would like to relay to your readers.

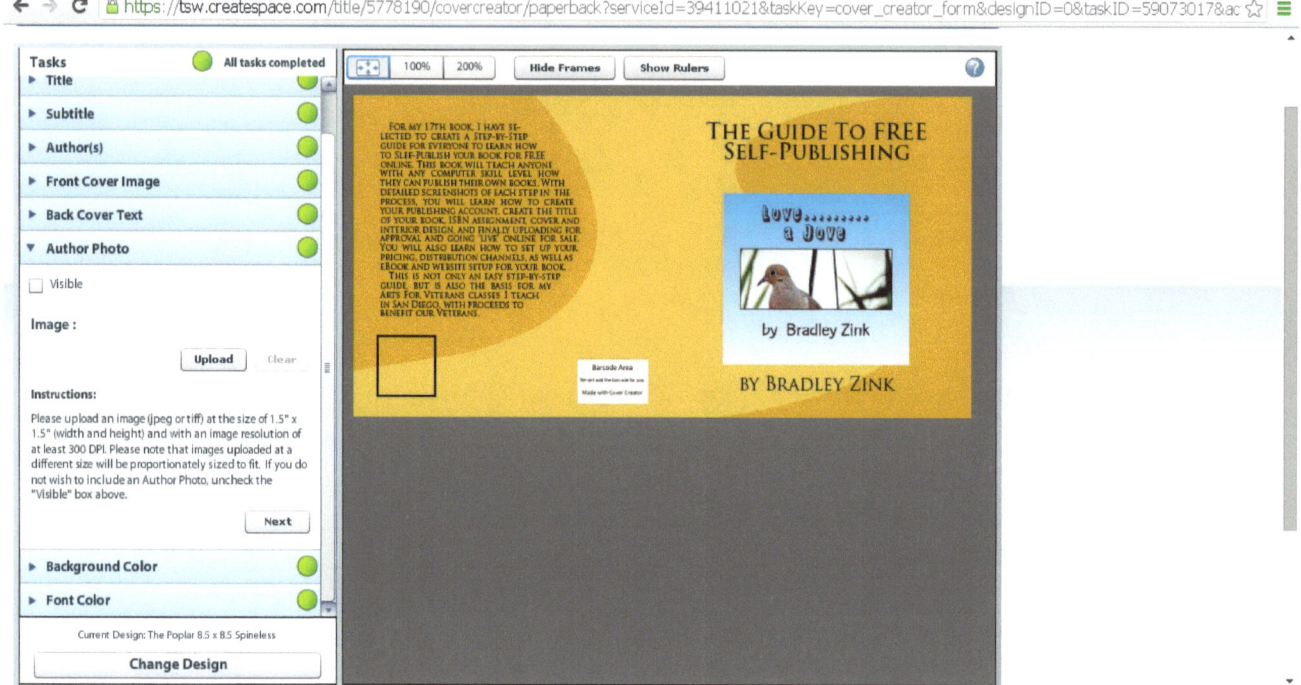

Cover Author Image

You have the option to either include or not an author image. Simply upload your picture, or uncheck the Visible box.

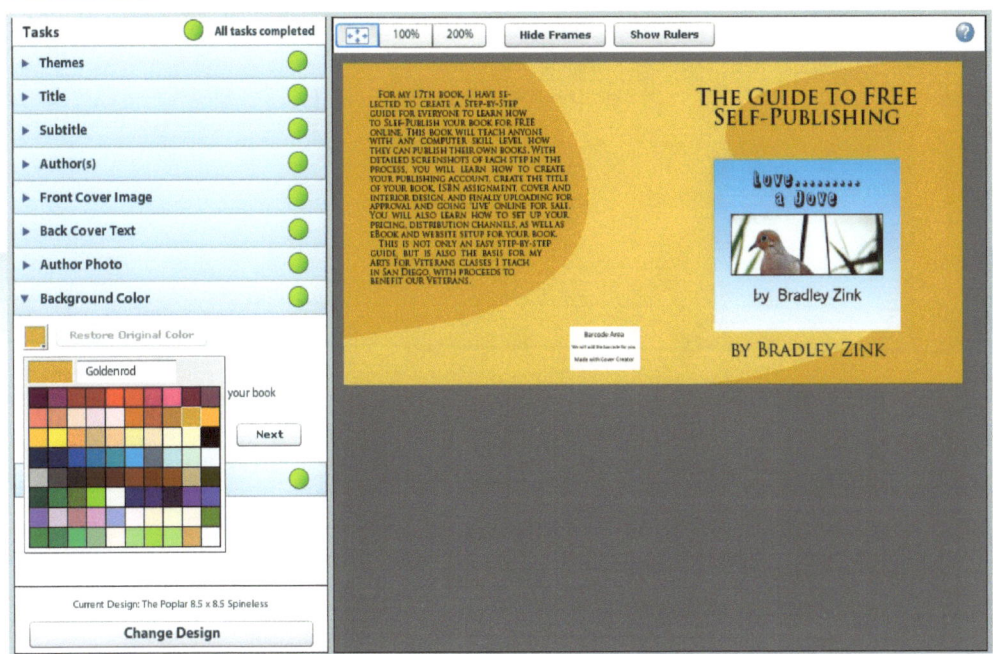

Cover Background Color

You can select from a wide array of colors for the Cover Background Color. Test several different colors to see which best suits your book.

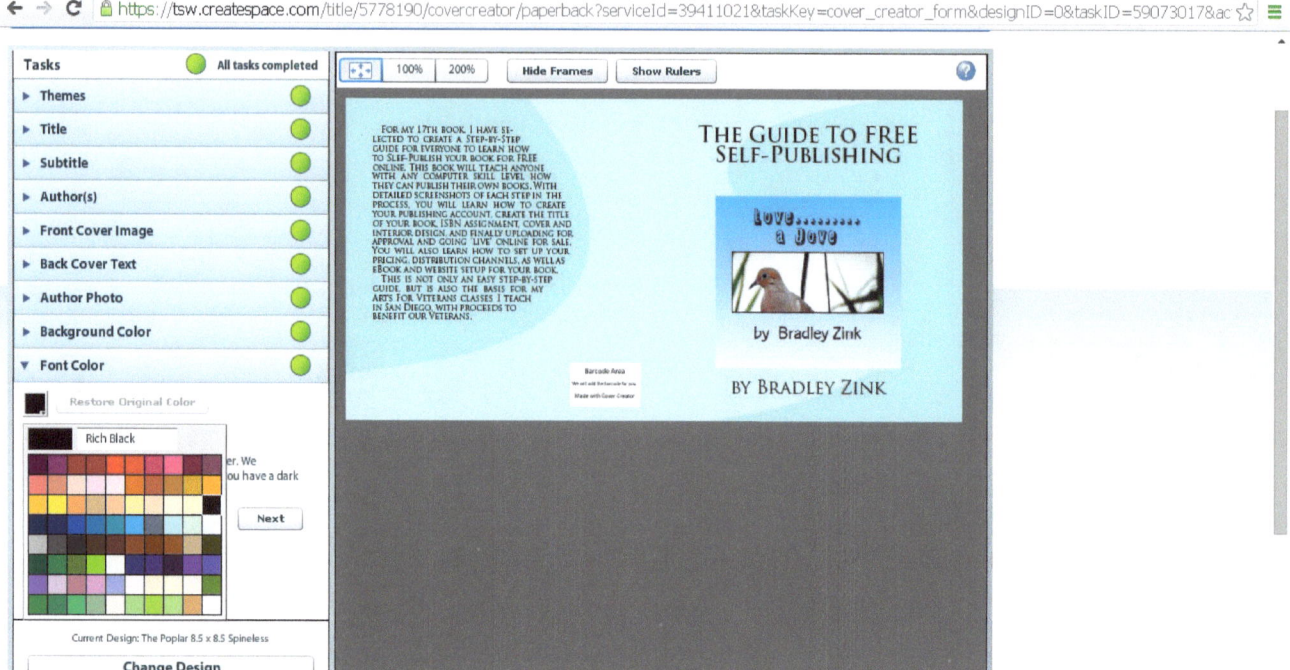

Cover Font Color

You can also choose from an array of Font Colors for your cover. Again, test several colors to see which best suits your book.

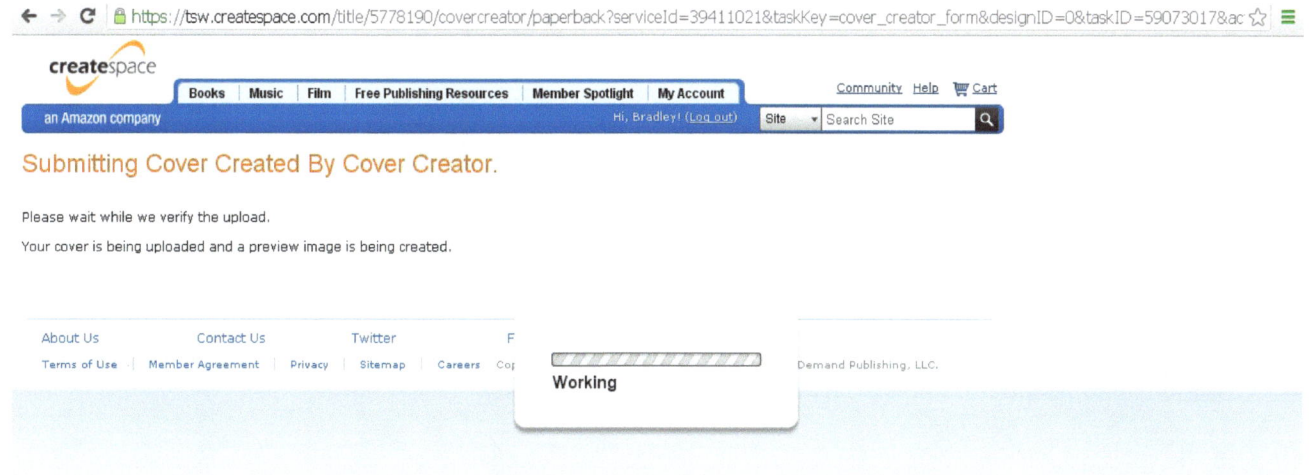

Cover Submit

Once you have completed the cover design, submit it for review. Once uploaded, you can select Full-Size Preview to get a good idea of how the finished cover will look.

For my 17th book, I have selected to create a Step-by-Step
guide for everyone to learn how
to Slef-Publish your book for FREE
online. This book will teach anyone
with any computer skill level how
they can publish their own books. With
detailed screenshots of each step in the
process, you will learn how to create
your publishing account, create the title
of your book, ISBN assignment, cover and
interior design, and finally uploading for
approval and going 'live' online for sale.
You will also learn how to set up your
pricing, distribution channels, as well as
ebook and website setup for your book.
    This is not only an easy step-by-step
guide, but is also the basis for my
Arts For Veterans classes I teach
in San Diego, with proceeds to
benefit our Veterans.

THE GUIDE TO FREE SELF-PUBLISHING

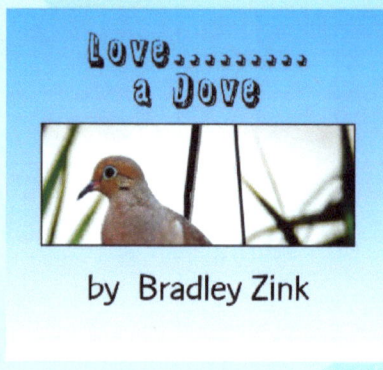

BY BRADLEY ZINK

Barcode Area

We will add the barcode for you.

Made with Cover Creator

Cover Full-size Preview

The Full-size preview will give you an idea of how the finished book cover will look, as well as a larger view to proof for errors.

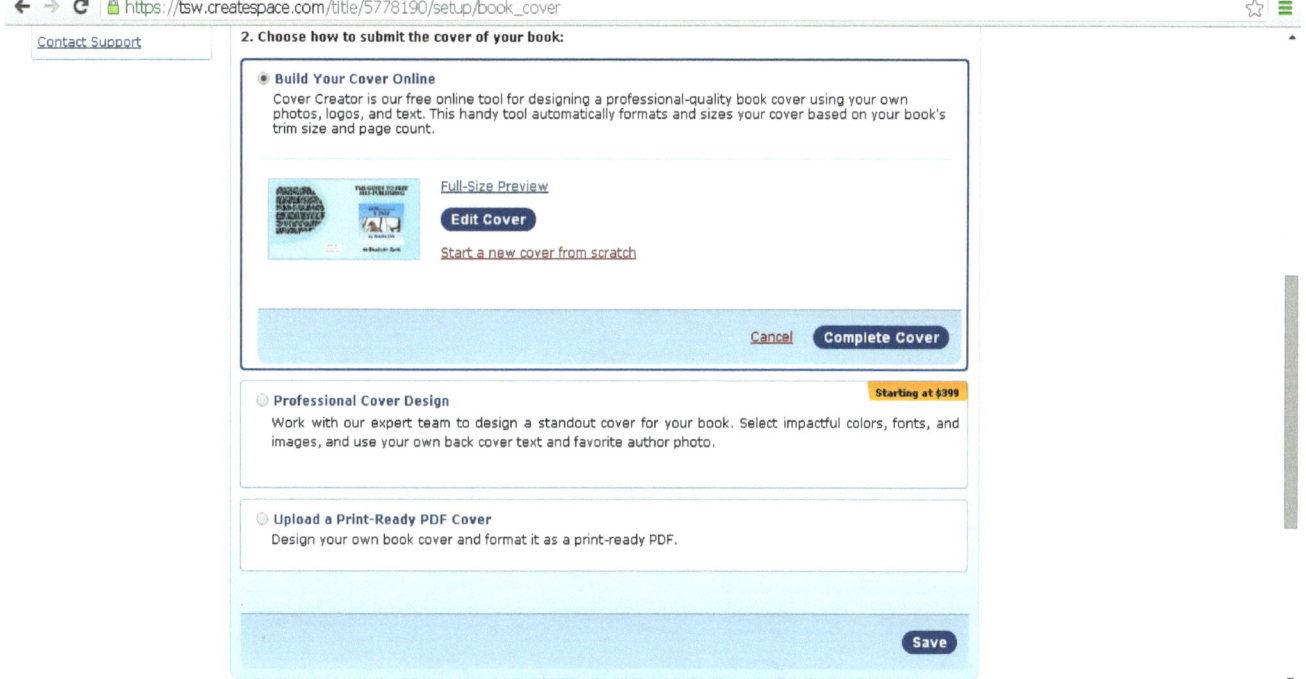

Cover Complete

Once you are pleased with the cover design, simply click Save then select Complete Cover.

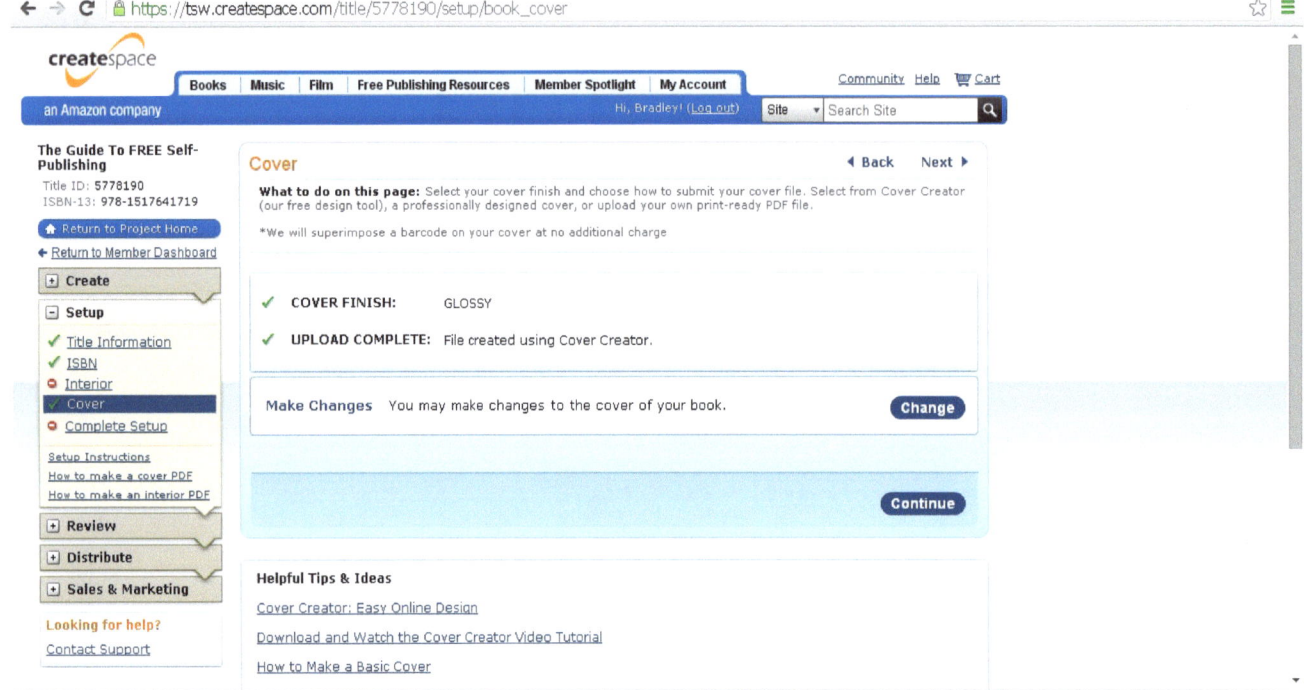

Cover Complete Cont.

Cover is completed, and now you can continue.

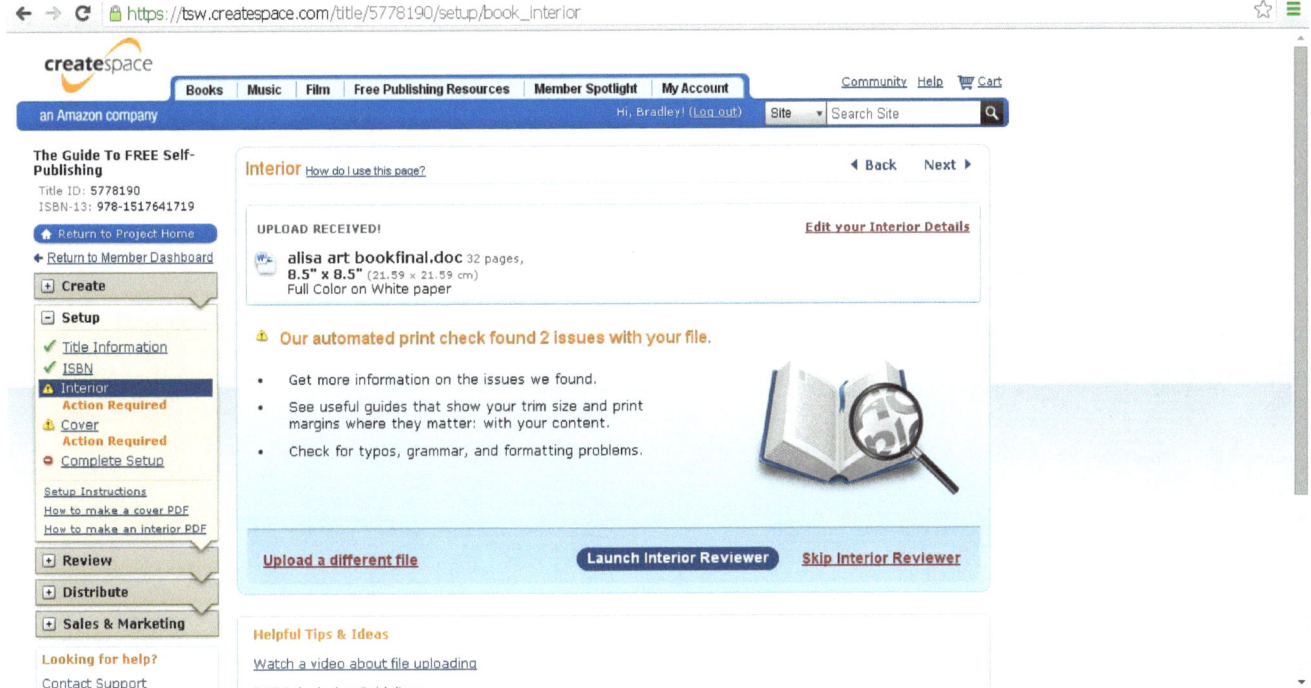

Print Check Issues

Sometimes, the Automated Print Check finds possible errors or issues with your interior. You can Check the issues with their Interior Reviewer program.

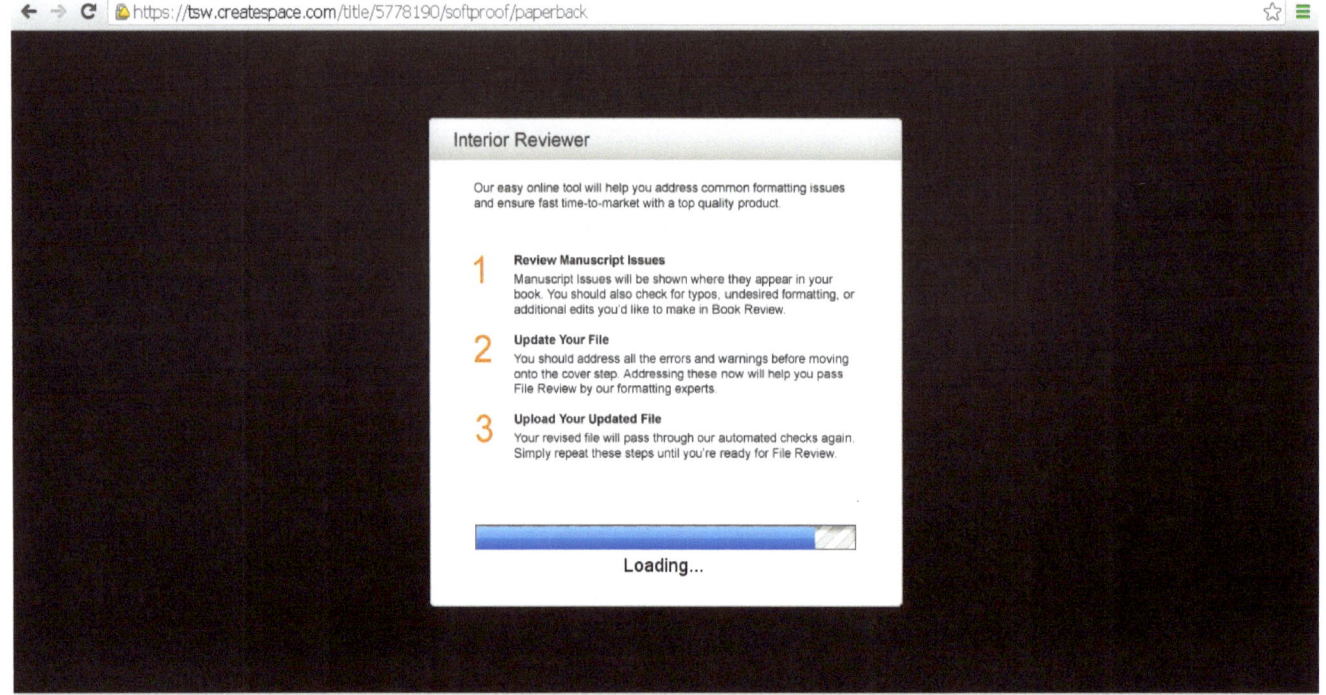

Interior Reviewer

Interior Reviewer will show you a digital look at how your book will look when printed. You can check any possible errors the Automated Print Check finds.

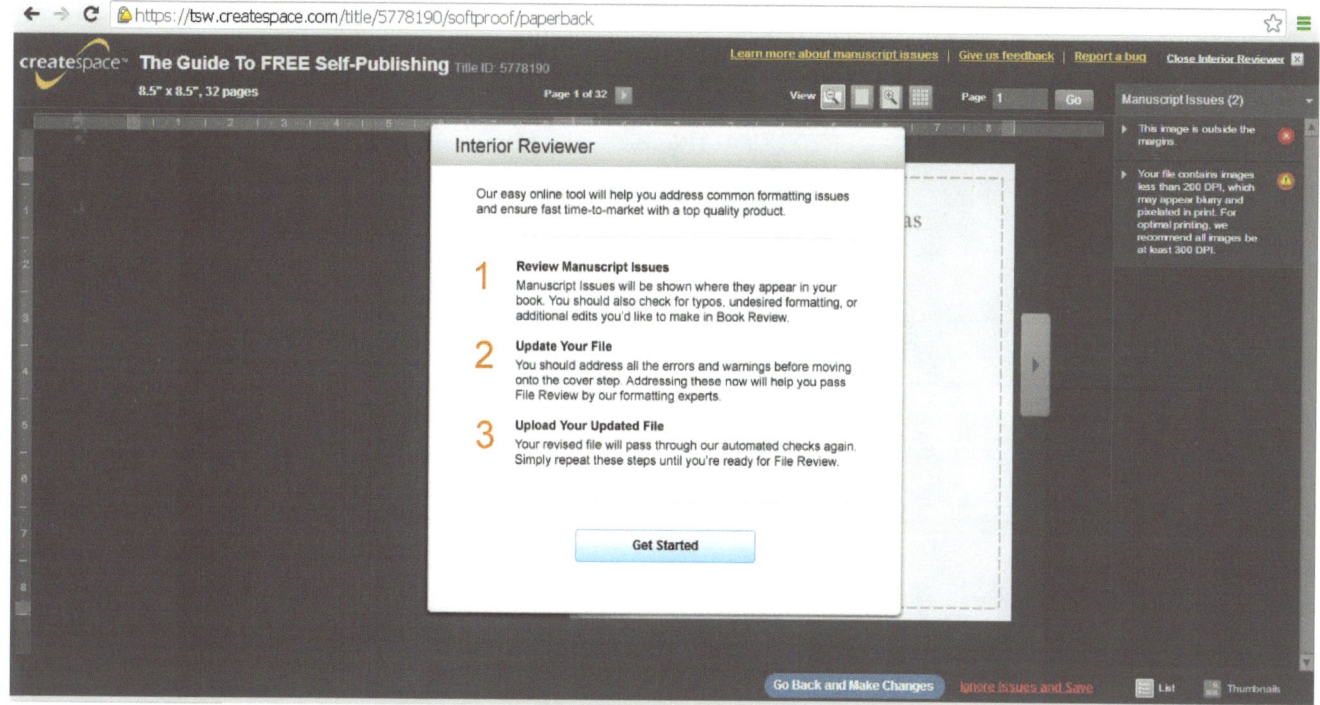

Interior Reviewer Start

With the Interior Reviewer, you will be able to check any detected errors in your book file. You will see how the book will look when printed, and can proof-read in a larger scale.

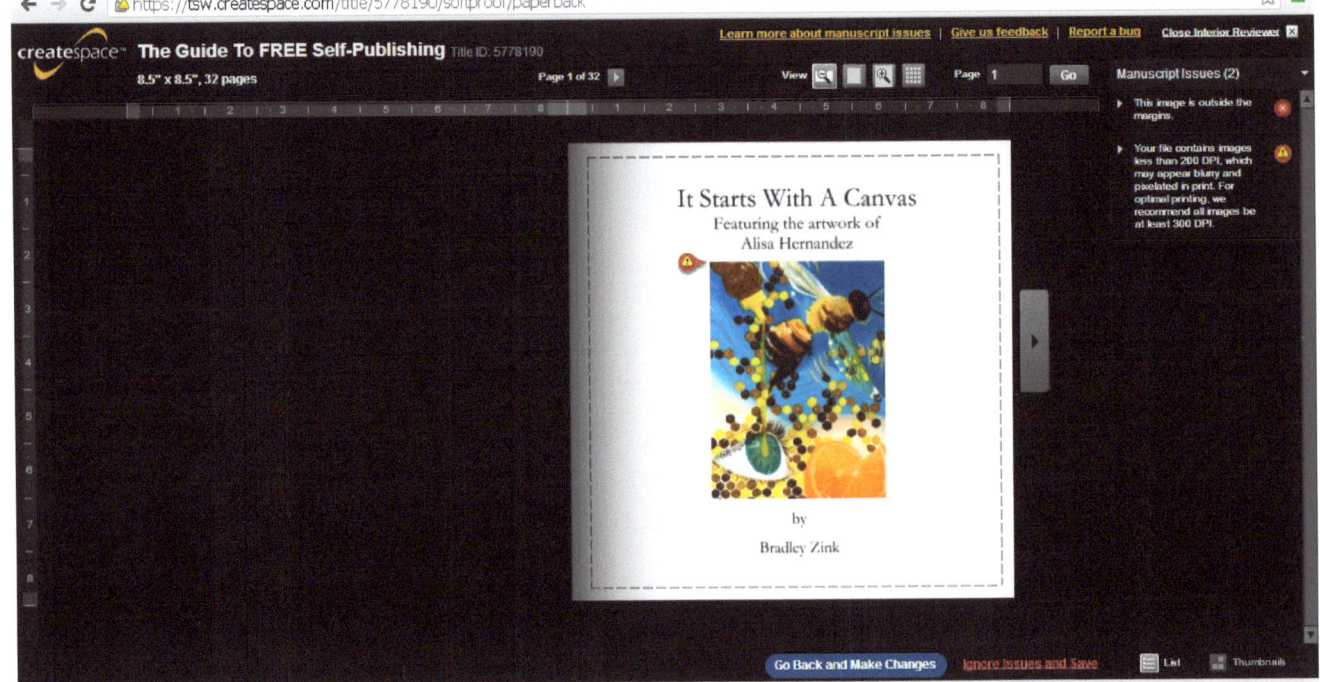

Interior Reviewer Errors

With the Interior Reviewer, it will highlight any detected errors, for you to review. You also get a page-by-page view of your book.

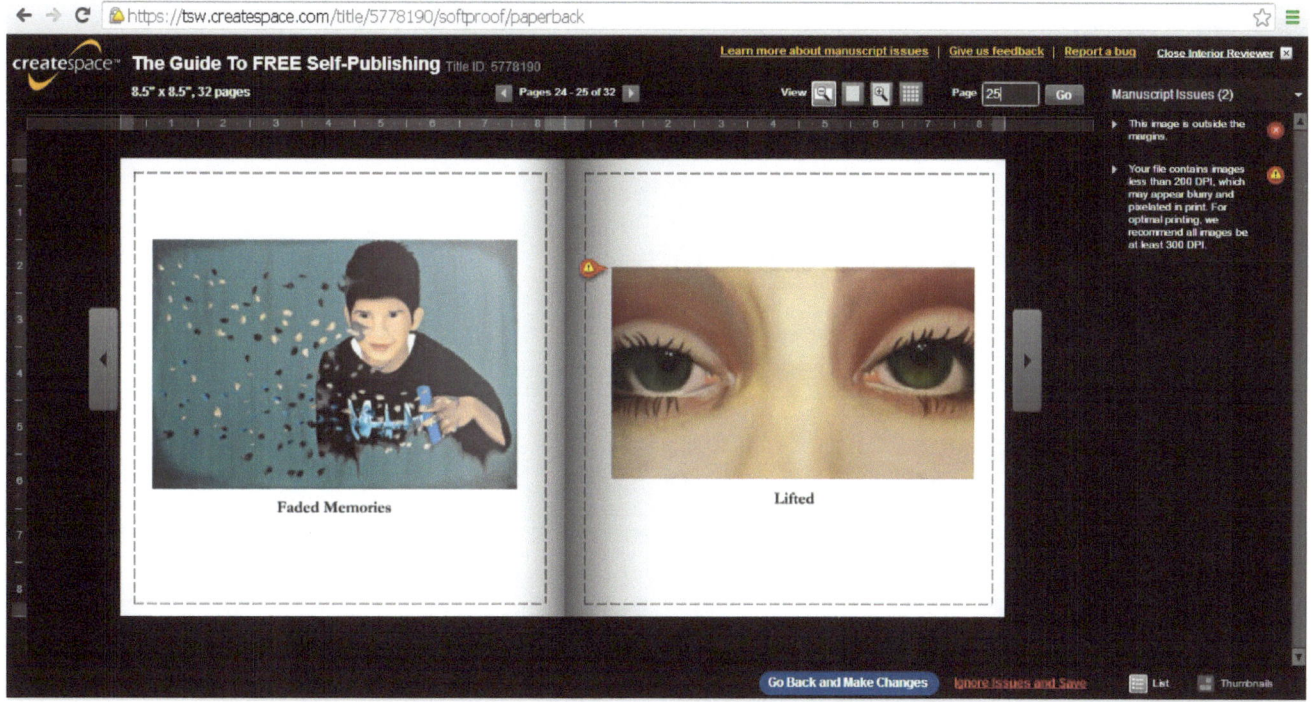

Interior Reviewer Errors Cont.

You can check highlighted errors to see what needs to be corrected before publishing.

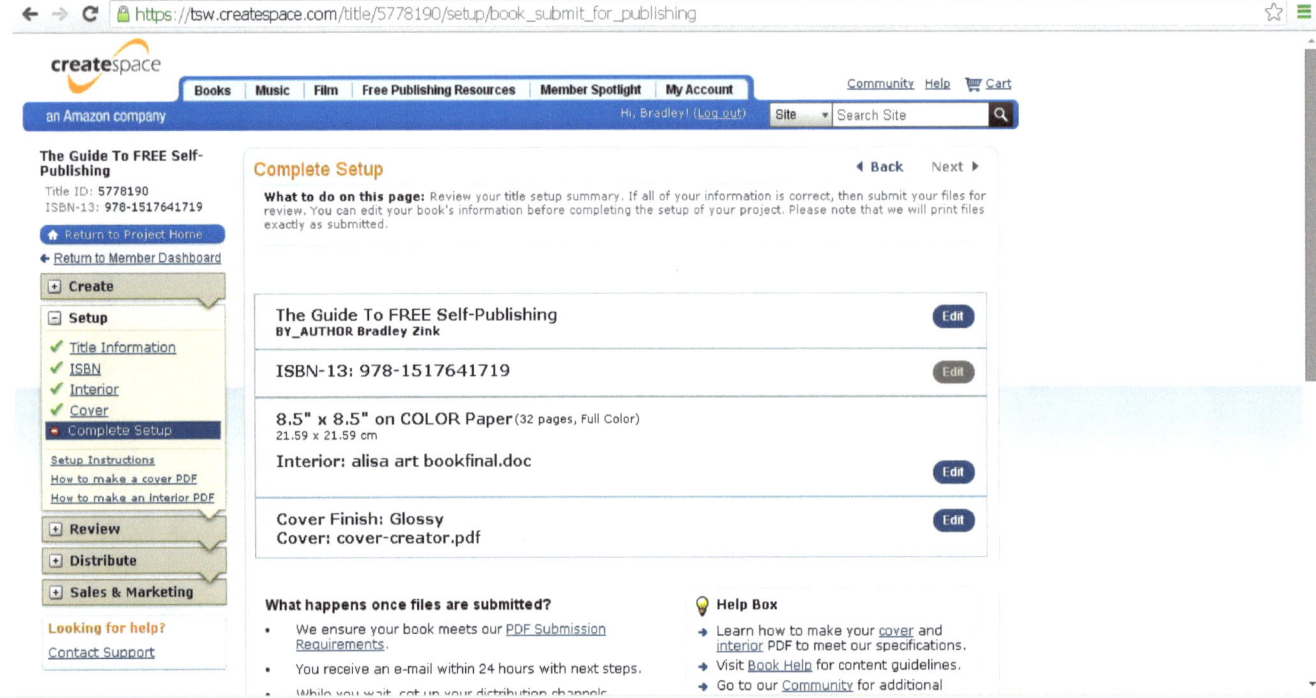

Complete Setup

Once you have finished the Interior Reviewer, you can go back to fix any errors, or continue to complete the setup process.

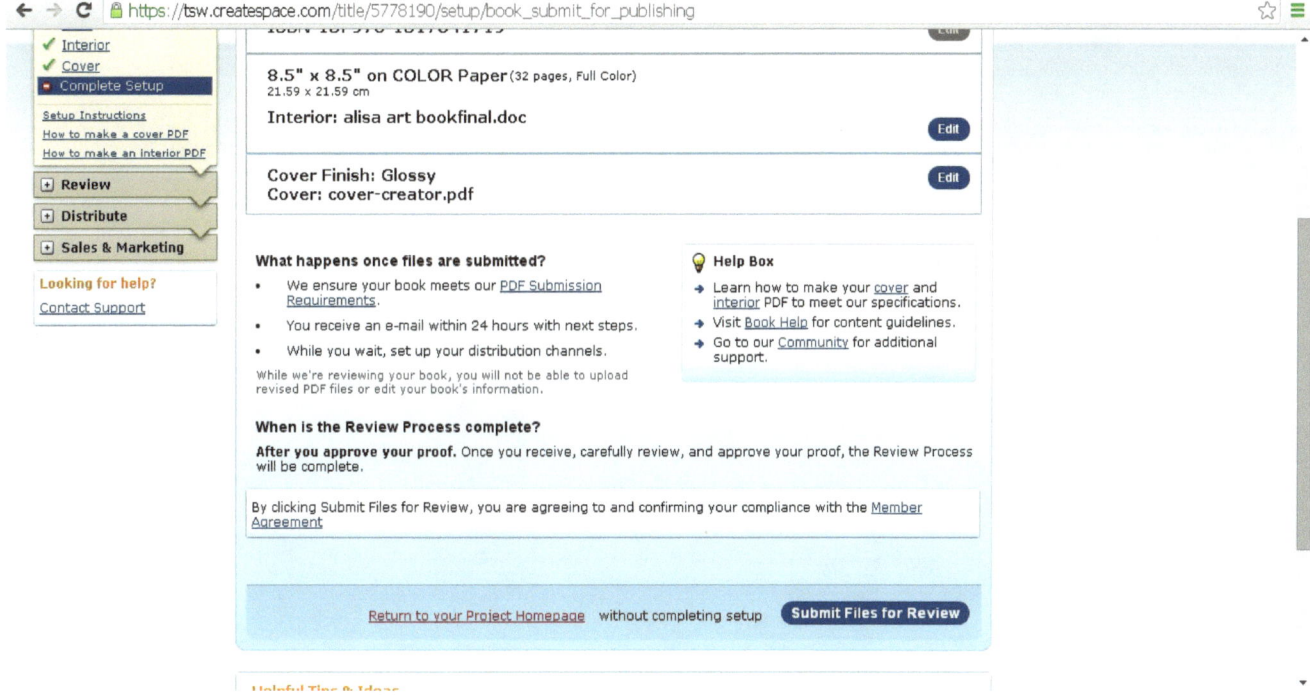

Complete Setup Cont.

If there are no errors to correct, simply Submit Files for Review.

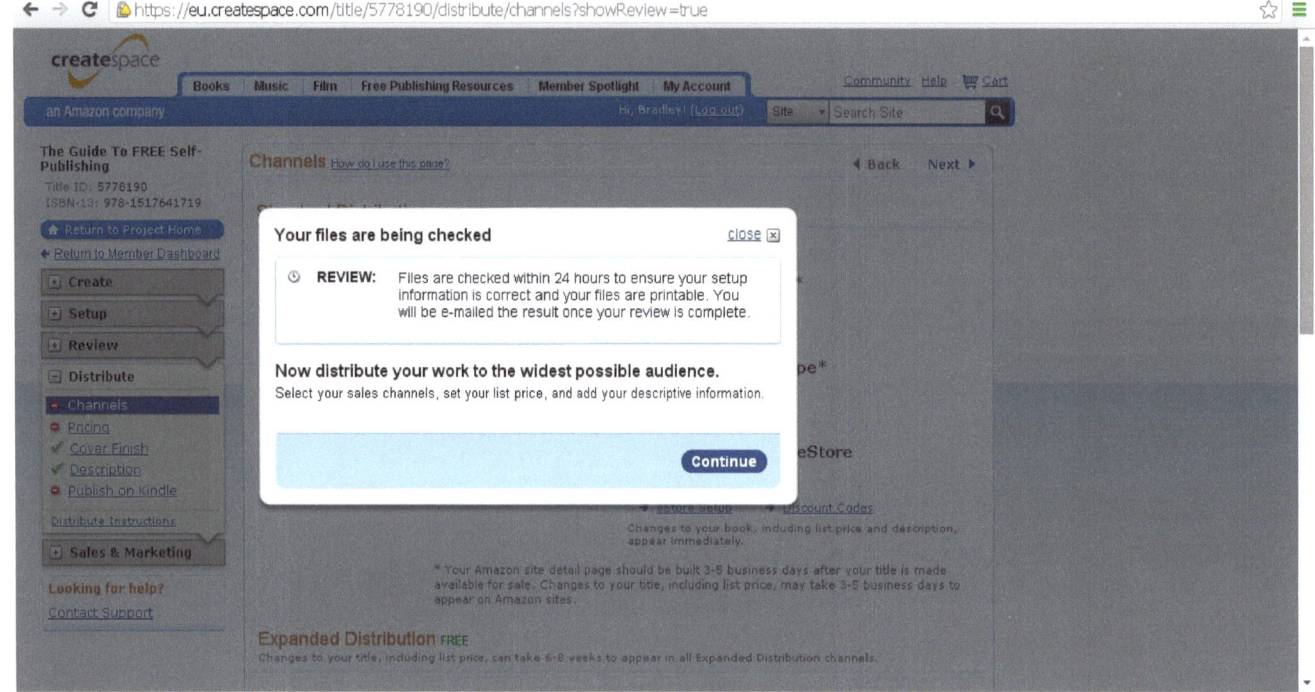

File Review Message

Files submitted for the Review Process are checked within 24 hours of submission, and you will be notified when the file review is completed. Next you can set up your Distribution Channels.

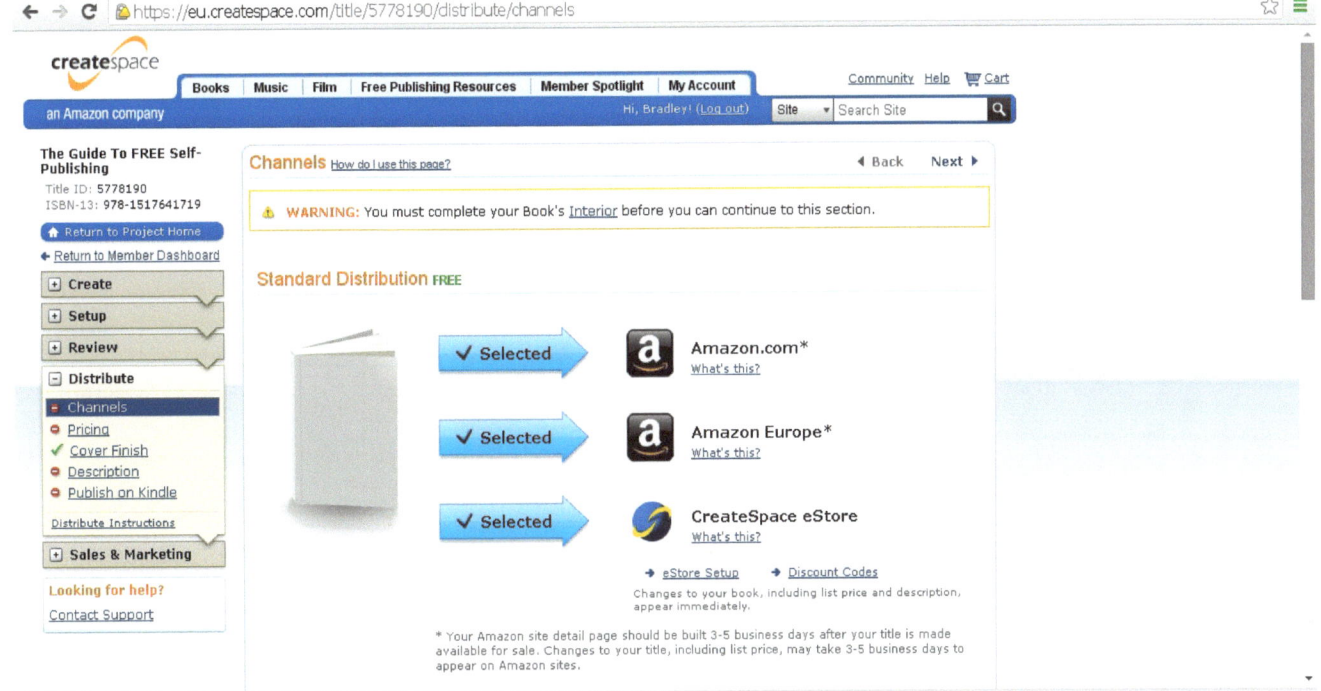

Distribution Channels

Your Distribution Channels are where your book will be available for purchase. The main channels are Amazon.com, Amazon Europe and your own CreateSpace eStore.

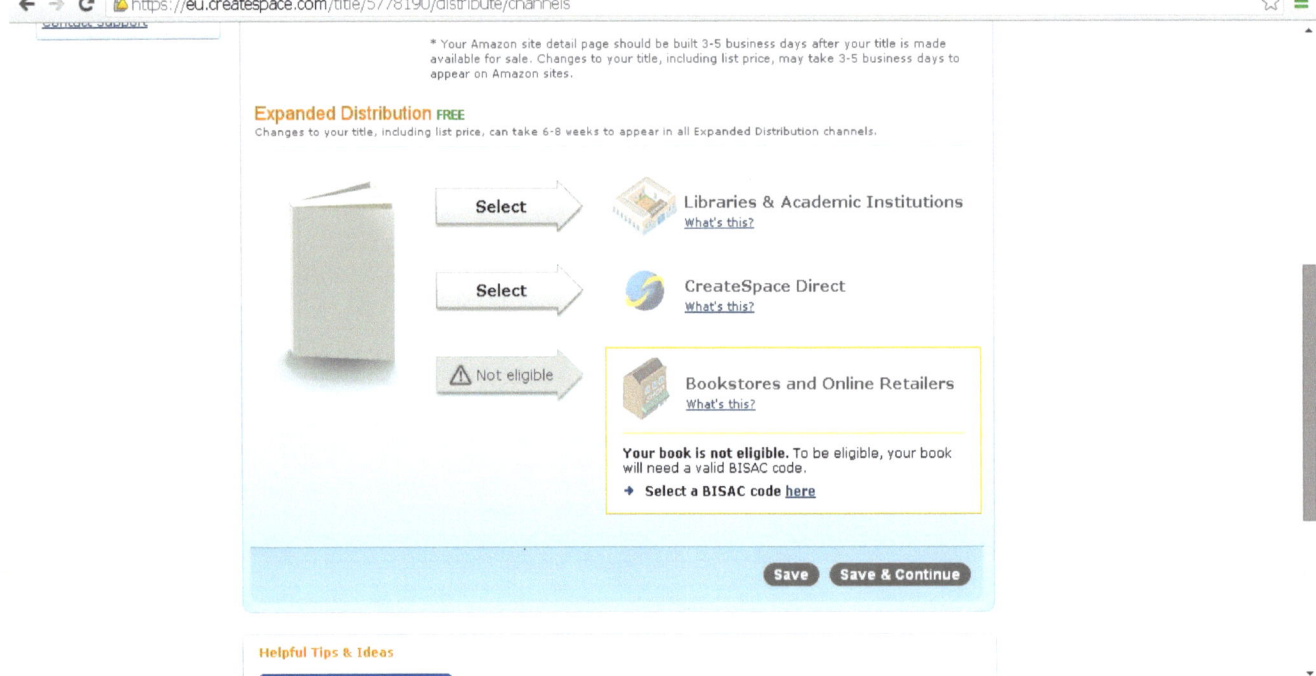

Expanded Distribution Channels

Your Expanded Distribution Channels are additional outlets to sell your book. These include Libraries & Academic Institutions, CreateSpace Direct, and Bookstores and Online Retailers.

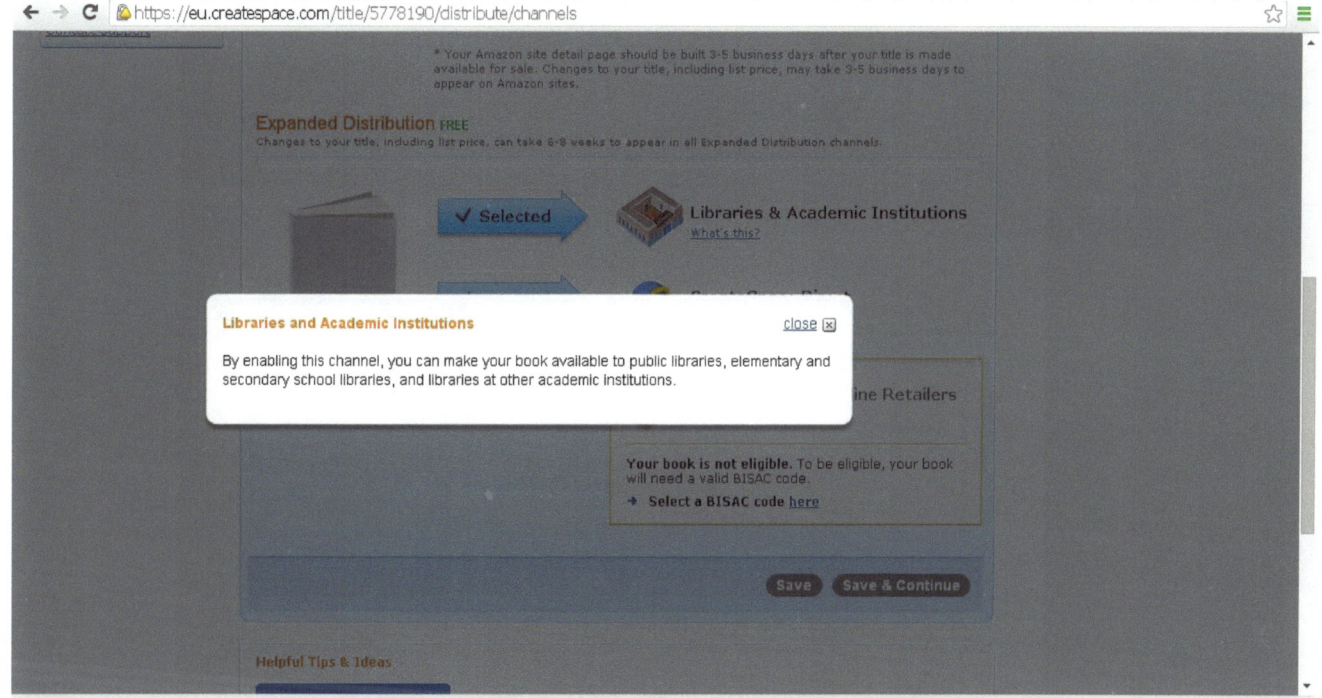

Library & Academic Distribution

By selecting Libraries & Academic Institutions, your book will be available to public libraries, elementary and secondary school libraries, and libraries at other academic institutions.

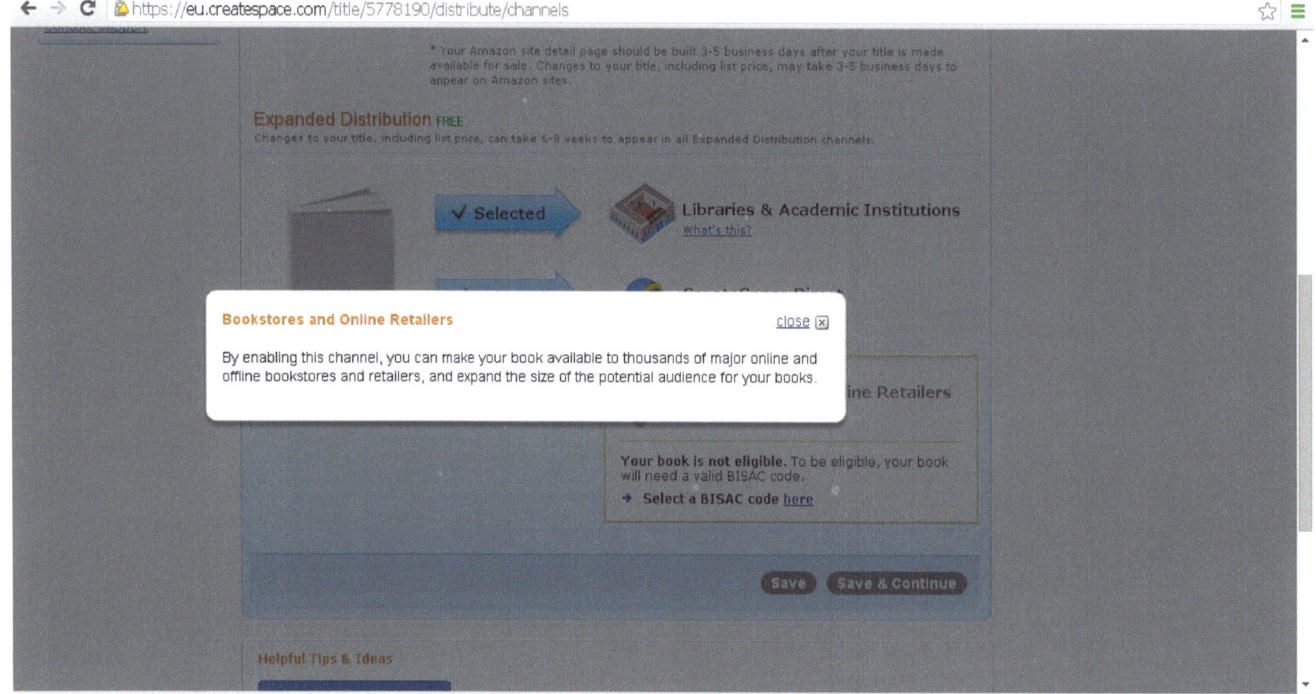

* Your Amazon site detail page should be built 3-5 business days after your title is made available for sale. Changes to your title, including list price, may take 3-5 business days to appear on Amazon sites.

Expanded Distribution FREE
Changes to your title, including list price, can take 6-8 weeks to appear in all Expanded Distribution channels.

✓ Selected   Libraries & Academic Institutions
What's this?

Bookstores and Online Retailers   close ⊠

By enabling this channel, you can make your book available to thousands of major online and offline bookstores and retailers, and expand the size of the potential audience for your books.

...ne Retailers

Your book is not eligible. To be eligible, your book will need a valid BISAC code.
→ Select a BISAC code here

Save   Save & Continue

Helpful Tips & Ideas

Bookstore & Online Retailer Distribution

By selecting Bookstores and Online Retailers, your book will be available to thousands of major online and offline bookstores and retailers, and expand the size of the potential audience for your book.

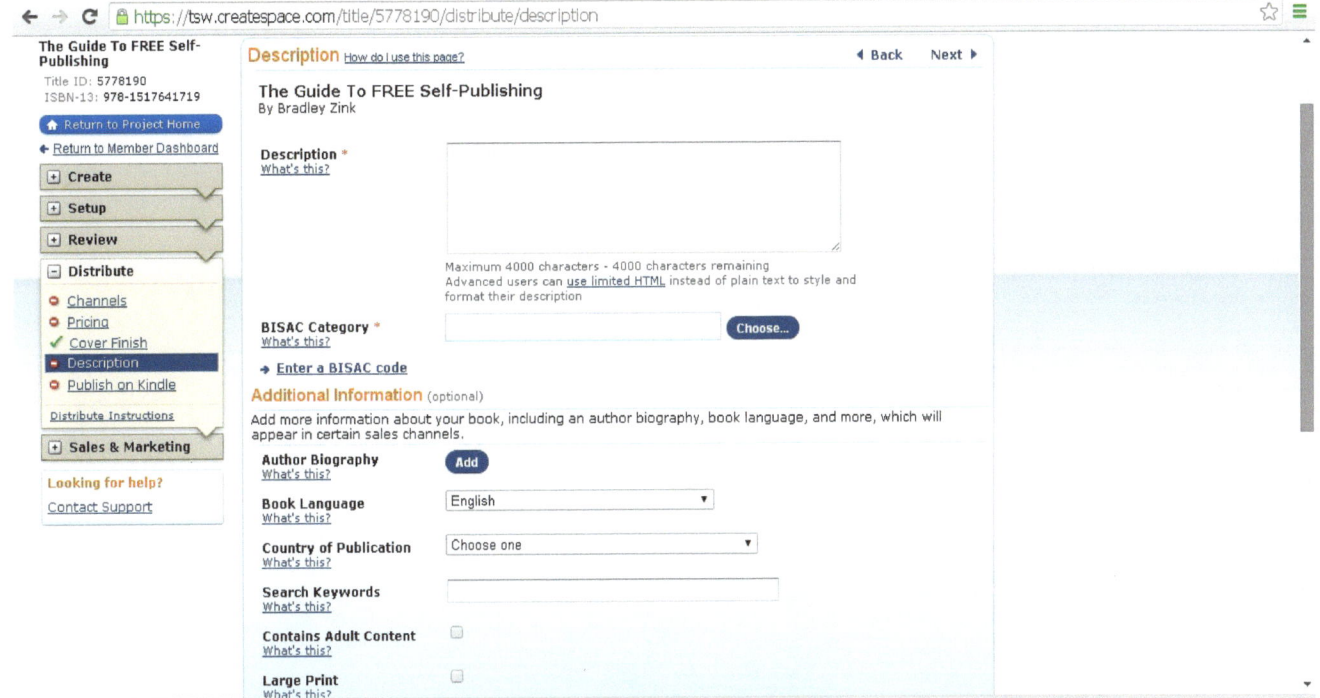

BISAC Code

To be available to Bookstores and Online Retailers, your book must have a BISAC Code assigned to it. Simply enter the description and assign the category for your book to be assigned the code.

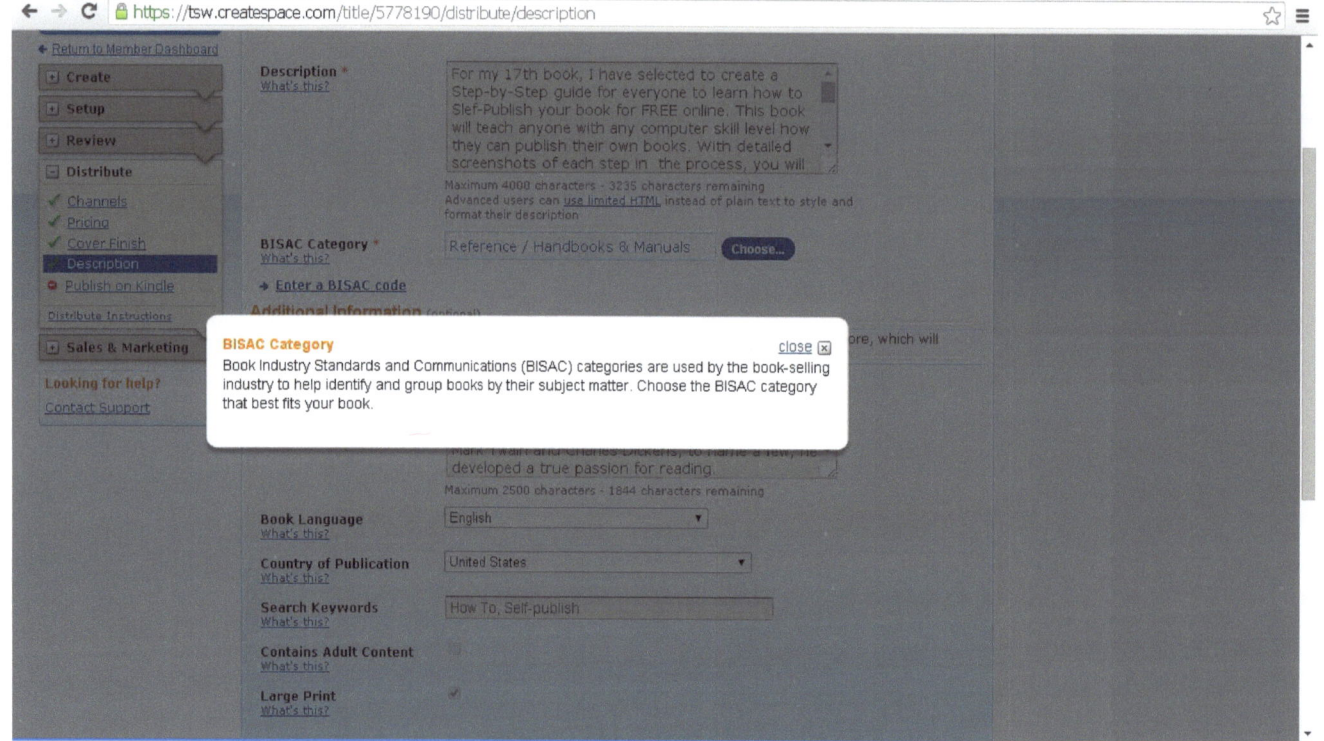

BISAC Definition

So what is BISAC? Book Industry Standards and Communications (BISAC) categories are used by the book-selling industry to help identify and group books by their subject matter.

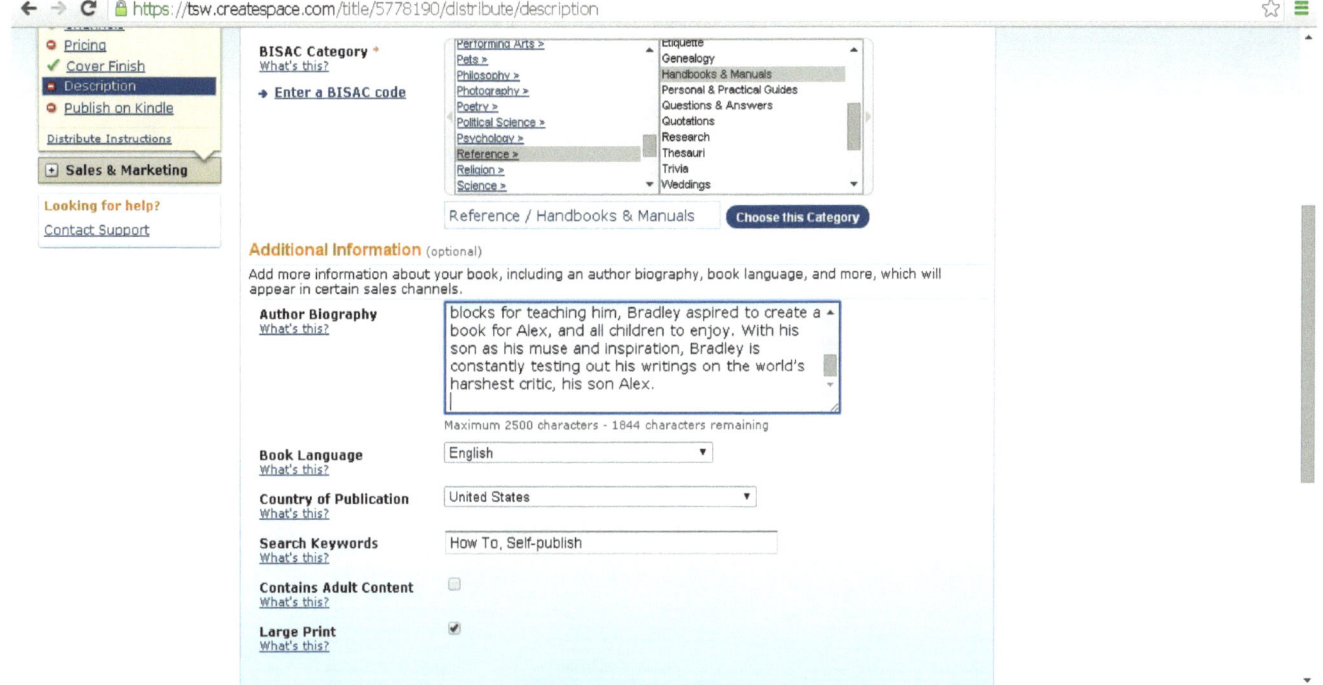

BISAC Cont.

You can also choose to include an author biography , as well as select the book language, Country of publication, keyword search terms. Be sure to check the boxes if your book contains Adult Content, or if it has Large Print.

Expanded Distribution Cont.

After you have selected your Expanded Distribution Channels, simply click Save and Continue.

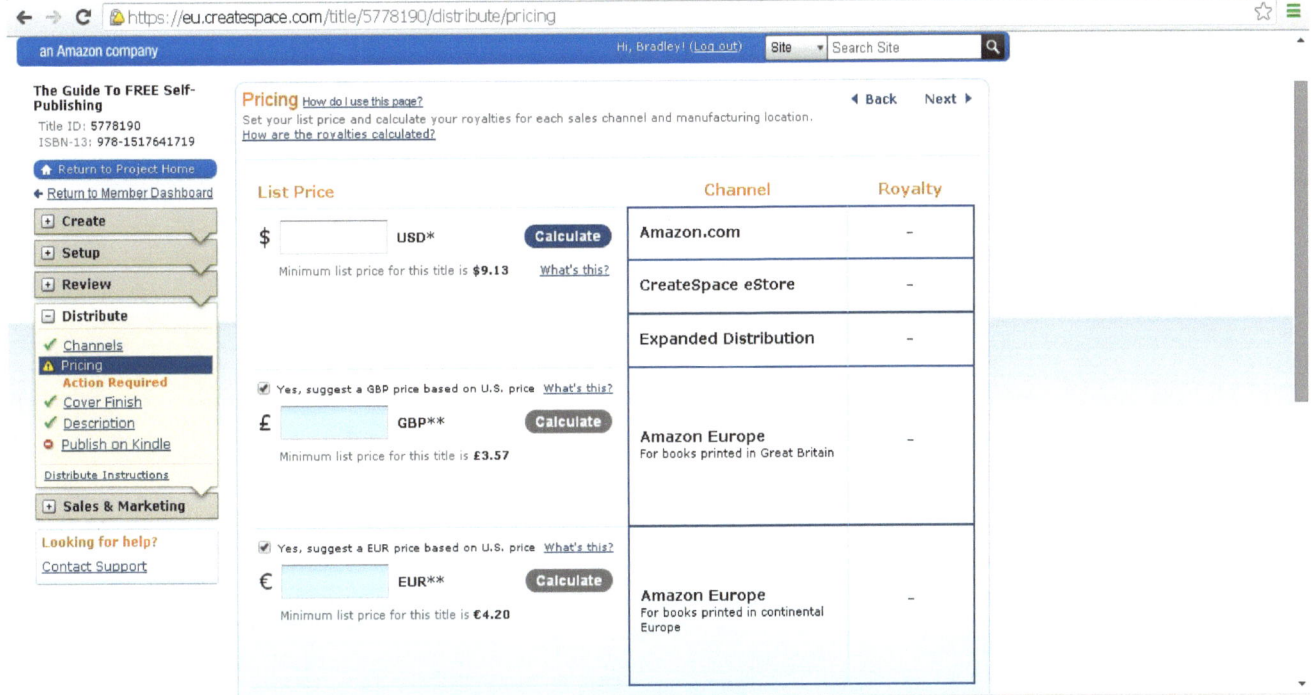

Pricing

Next you can set up the Pricing for our book. There is a Minimum list price preset by CreateSpace, based on size of book.

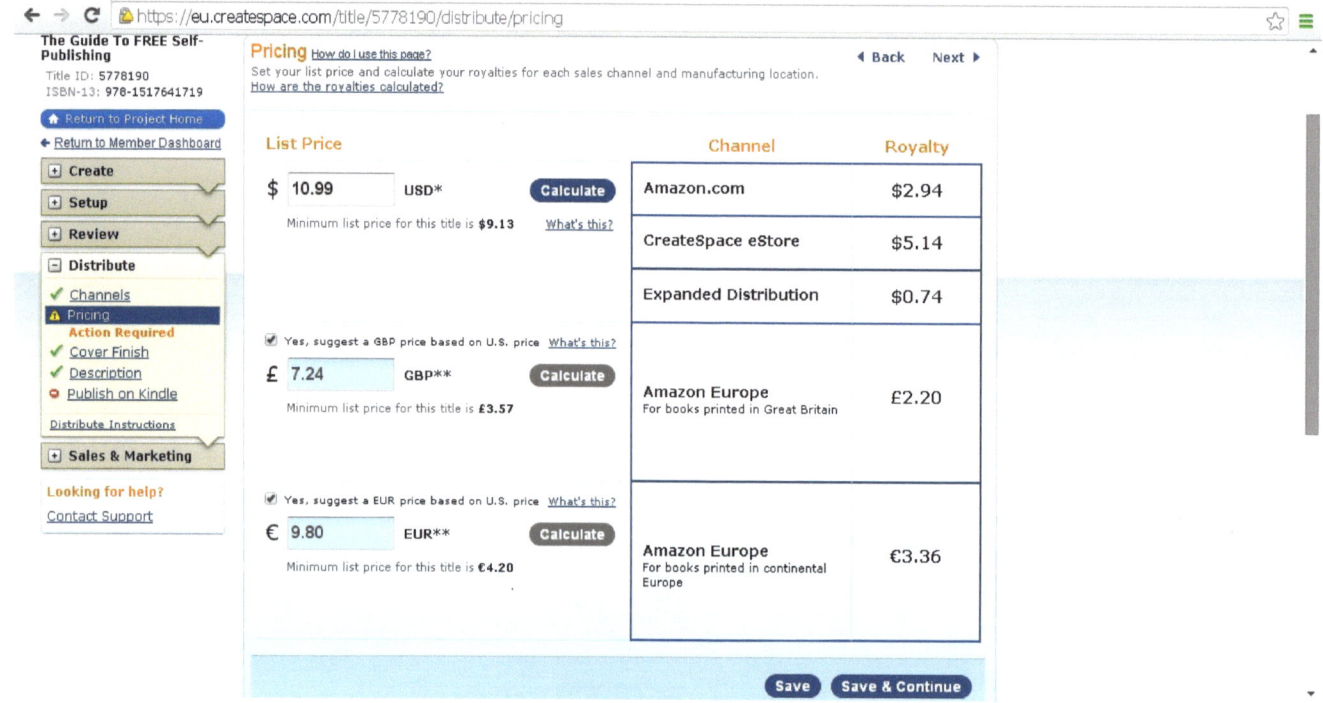

Pricing Cont.

Once you've chosen a price, it will show you a breakdown of your royalties per distribution channel.

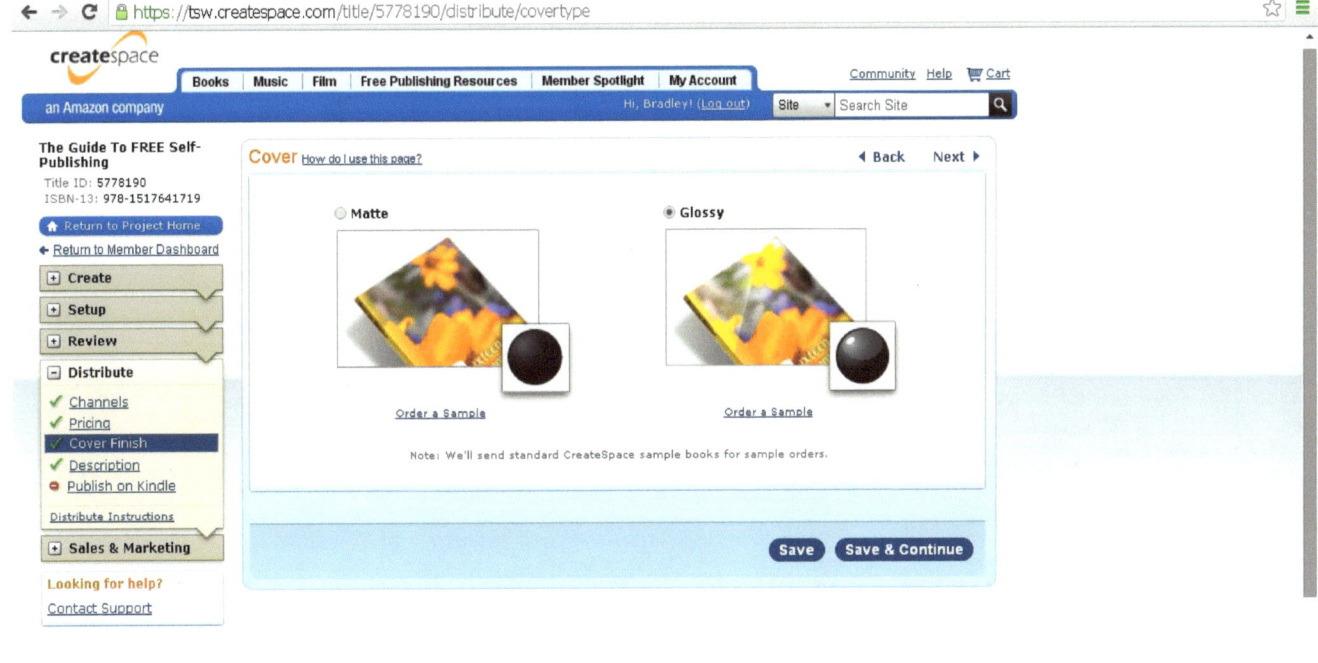

Cover Finish

For the Cover selection, you choose whether to have a Matte (flat finish) or Glossy (high shine) finish. Save and Continue.

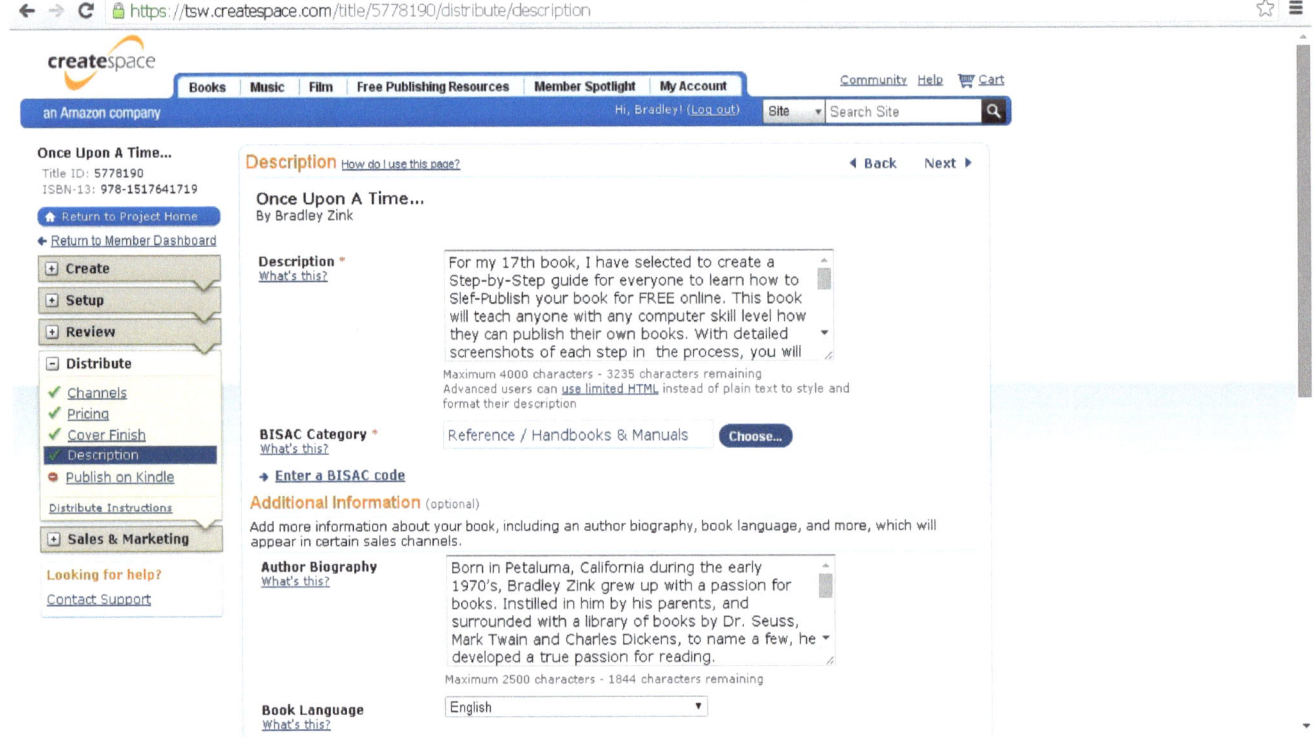

Description

The Description has already been filled in when you were assigning the BISAC code for your book. It's a good chance to proof the description one more time.

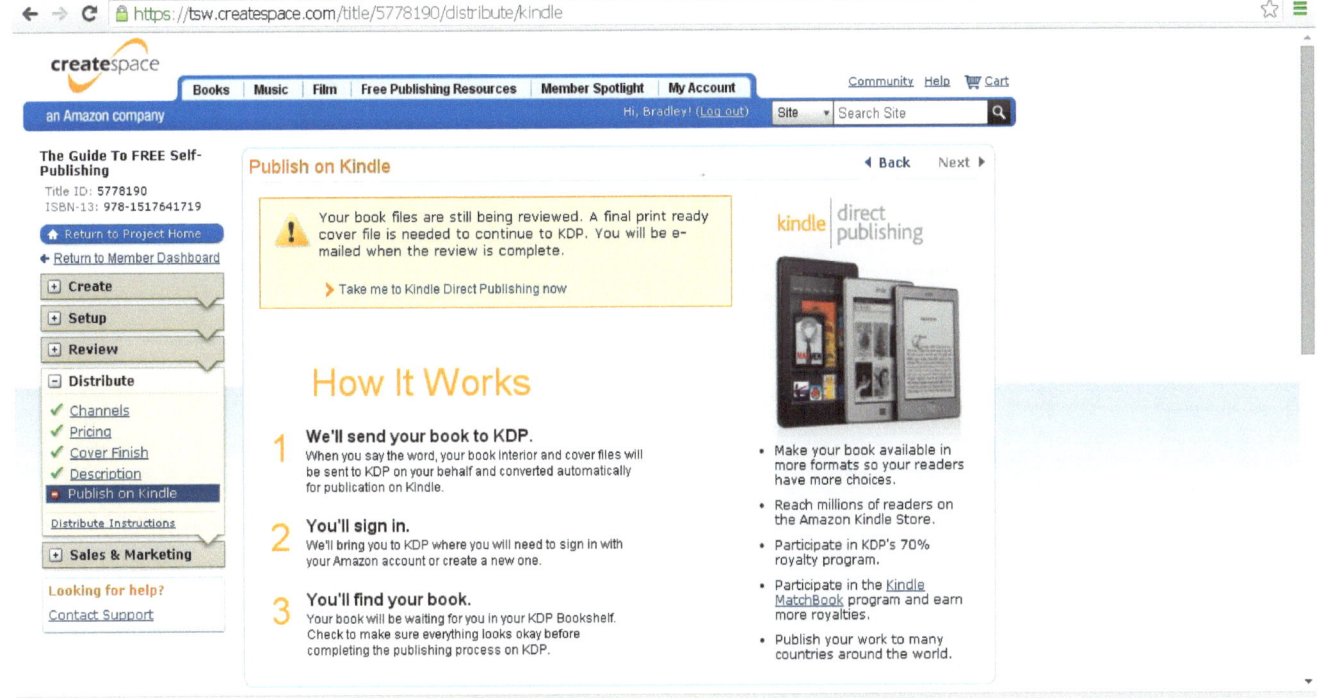

Publish on Kindle

Another great free option from CreateSpace is the ability to publish your book on Kindle. Follow the simple steps, and your book will be available as an eBook as well.

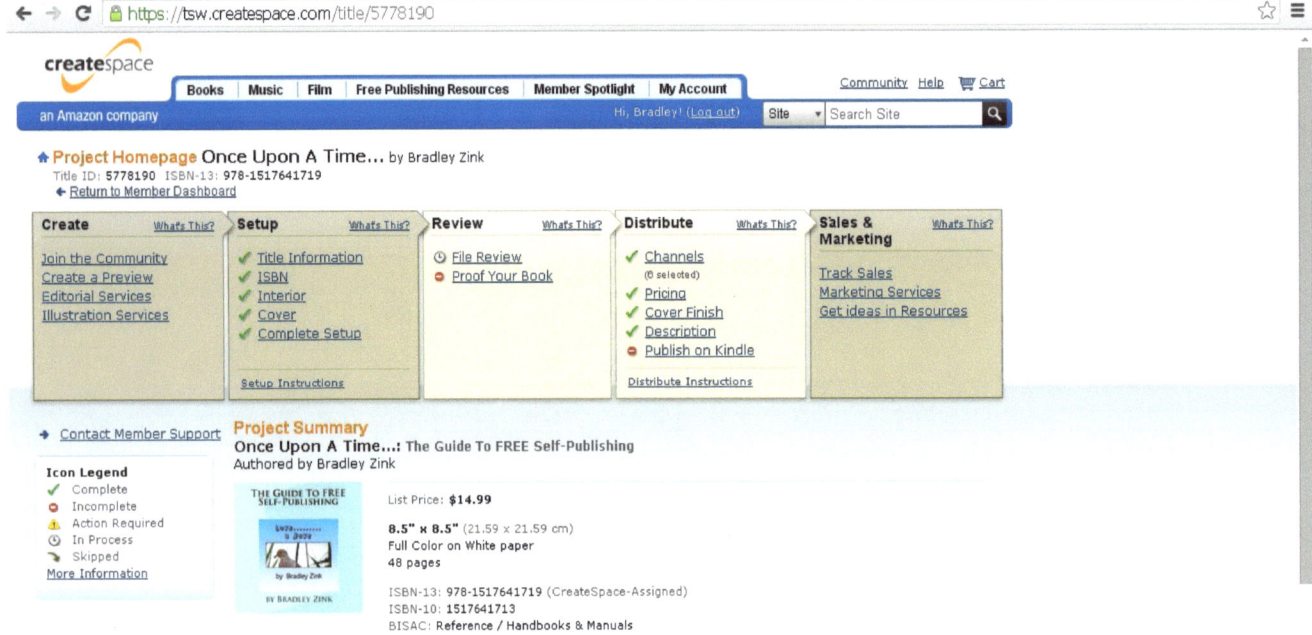

Project Homepage

Back at your Project Homepage, you will now see your book is in the File Review process. You will be notified once your book file has been reviewed. This is usually within 24 hours of submission.

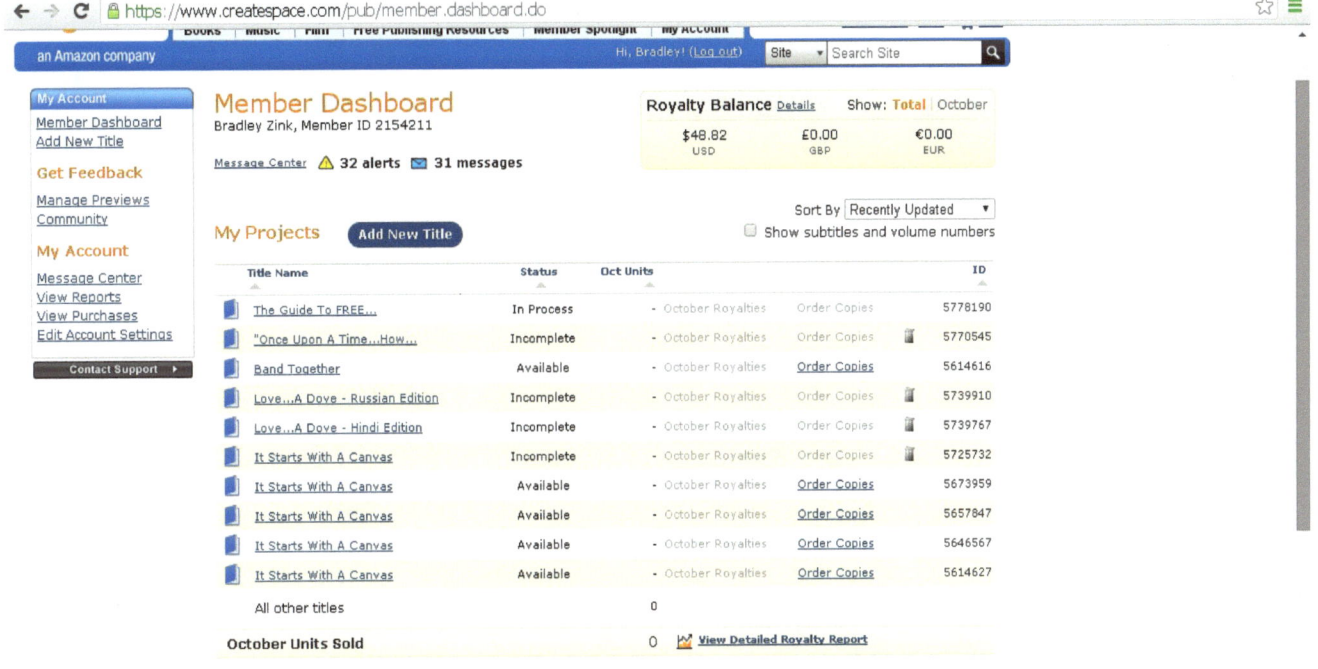

Member Dashboard In Process

Back at your Member Dashboard, you will now see the Status has changed to In Process. You will see a new message in the message center once your file review is complete.

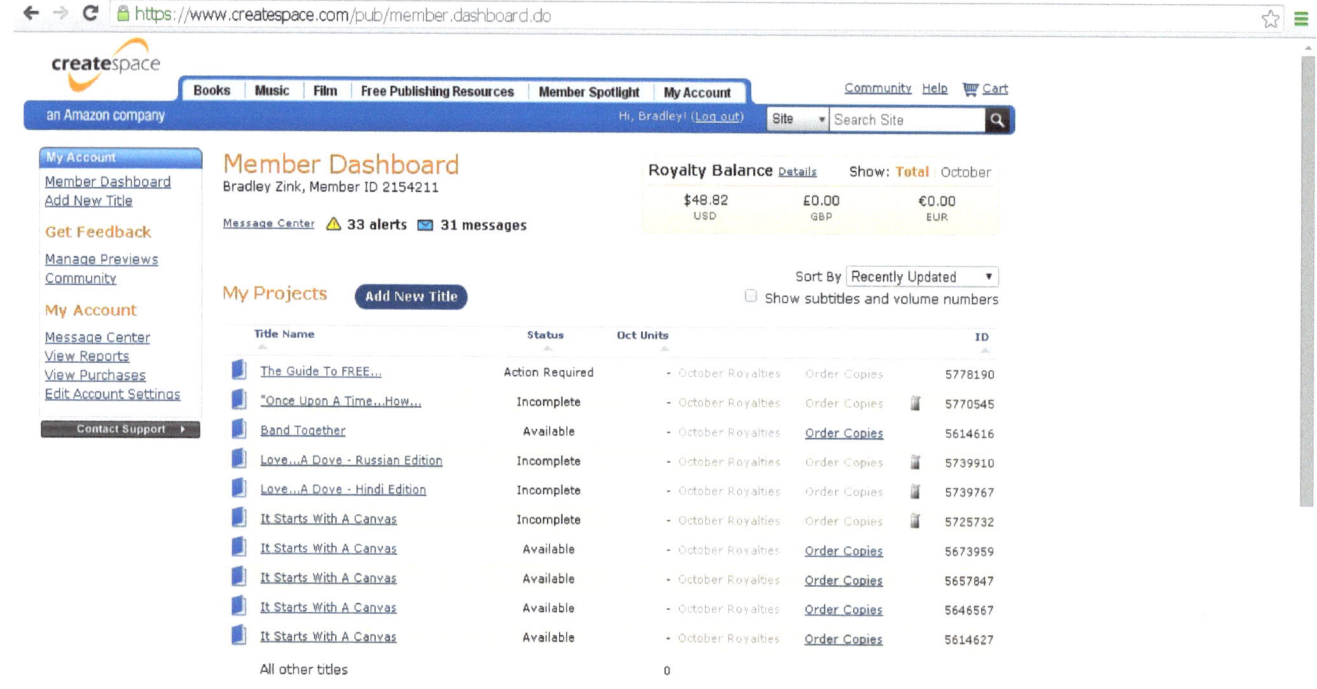

Action Required

Now that you have received notification that Action Required for your book file, go to your Member Dashboard and select your book listed as Action Required in the Status field.

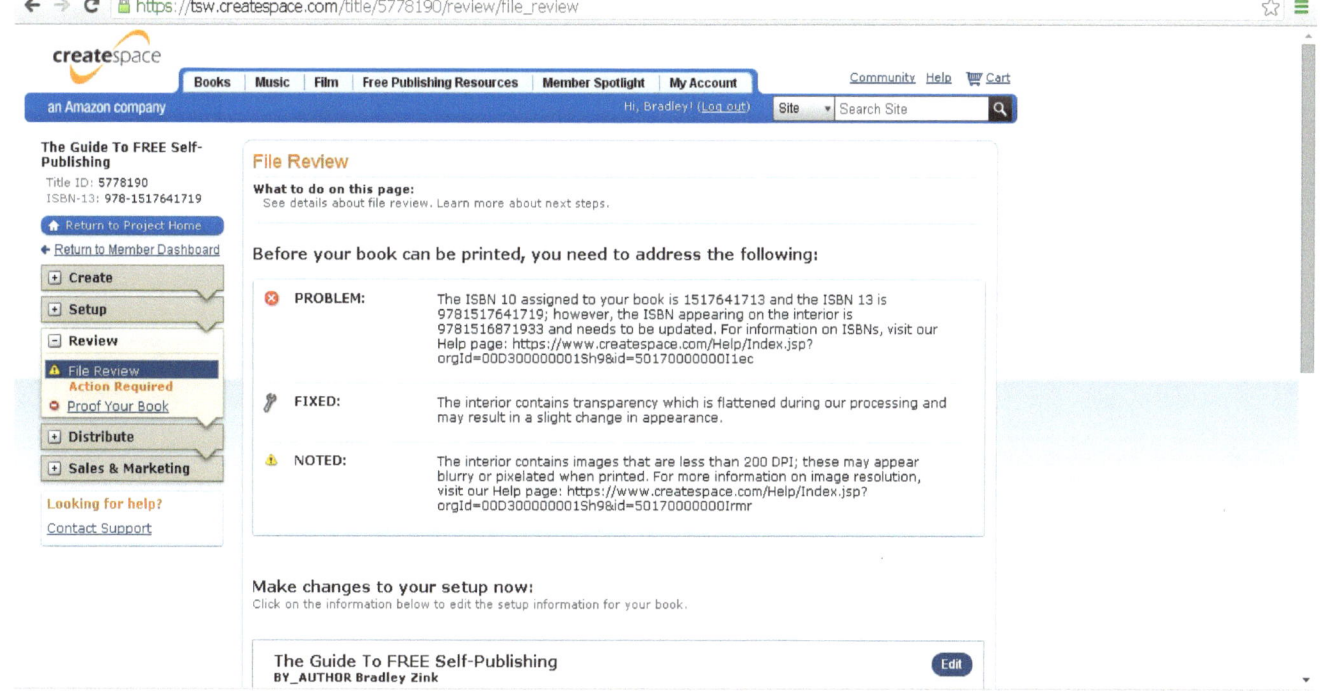

File Review Errors

If the File Review process detects any additional errors, that would prevent your book from properly printing, the issues will be listed. Simply fix the errors and re-submit your file for review.

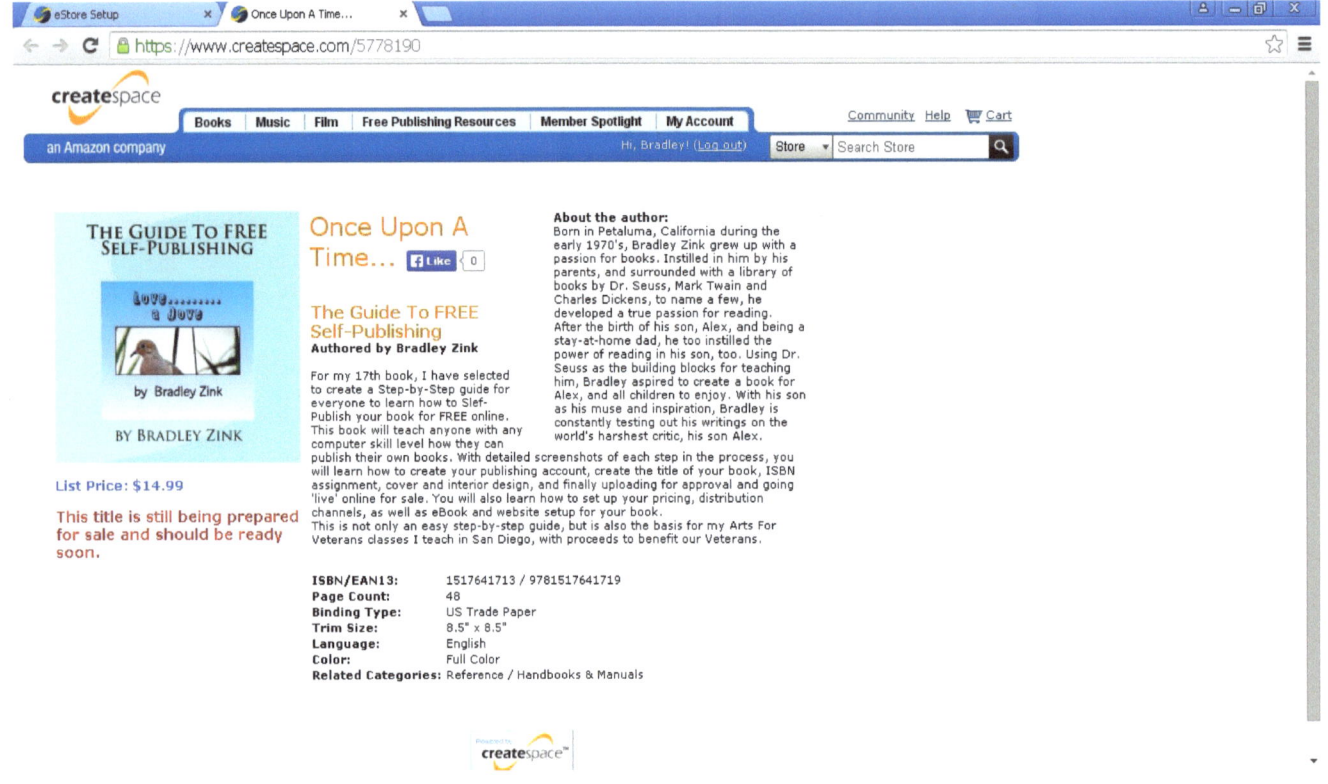

eStore Setup

While your book is still under review, your dedicated eStore page will display but not allow sales.

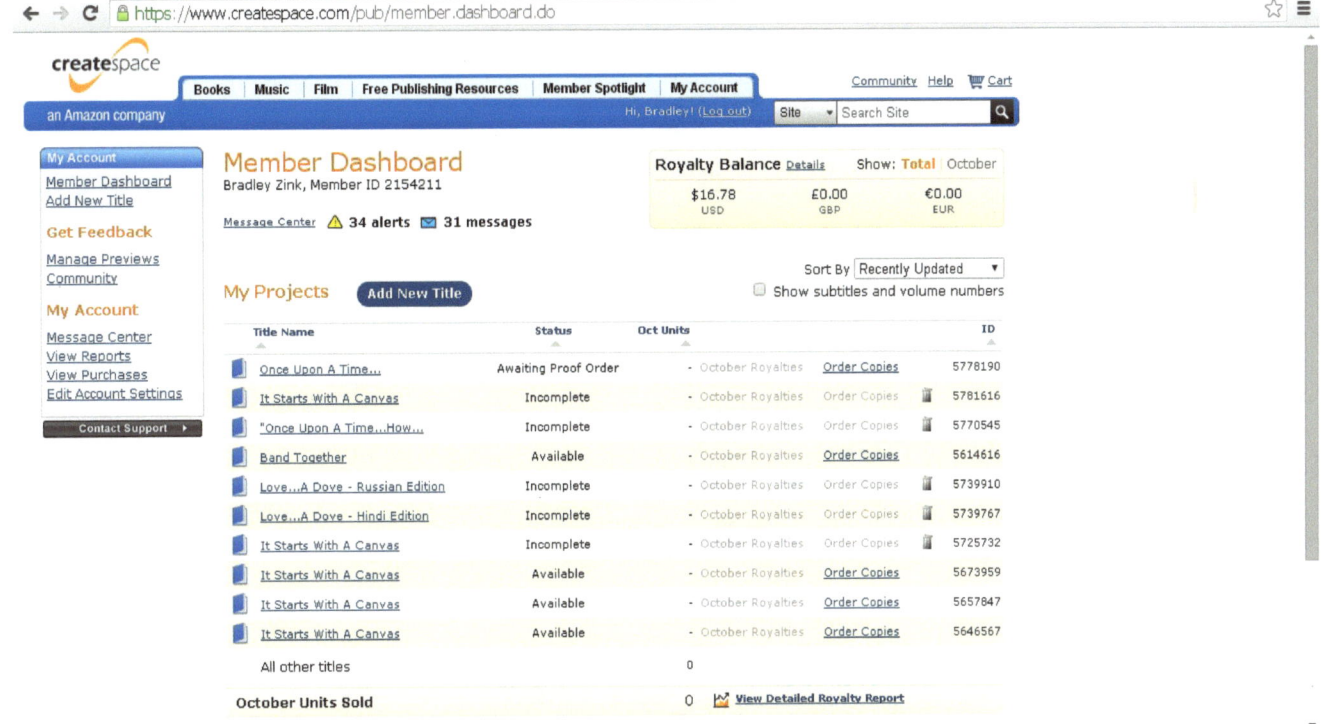

Awaiting Proof

Once your file has been approved during the File Review process, your Member Dashboard will display your book Status as Awaiting Proof Order. Click on your book to go through the Proof process.

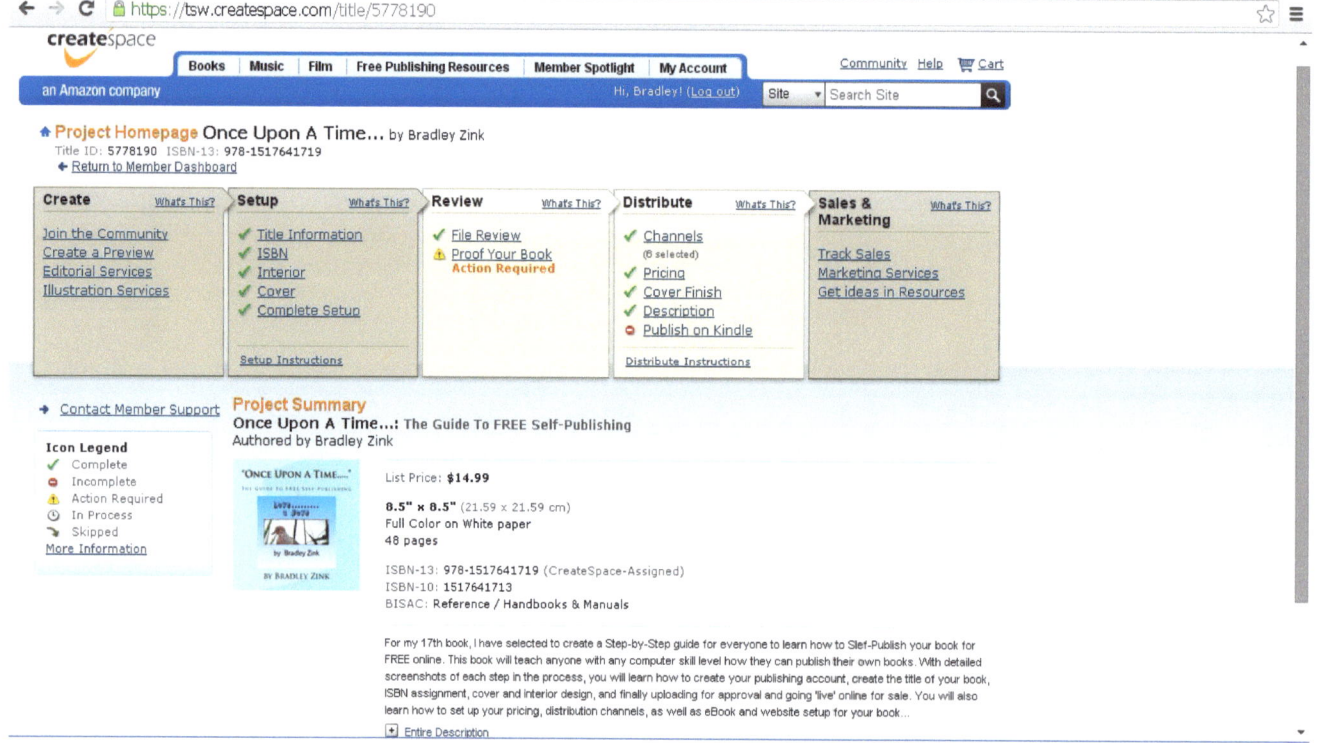

Proof Your Book

Next is the process of Proofing your book. There are a couple of options to select on the Proof Your Book page.

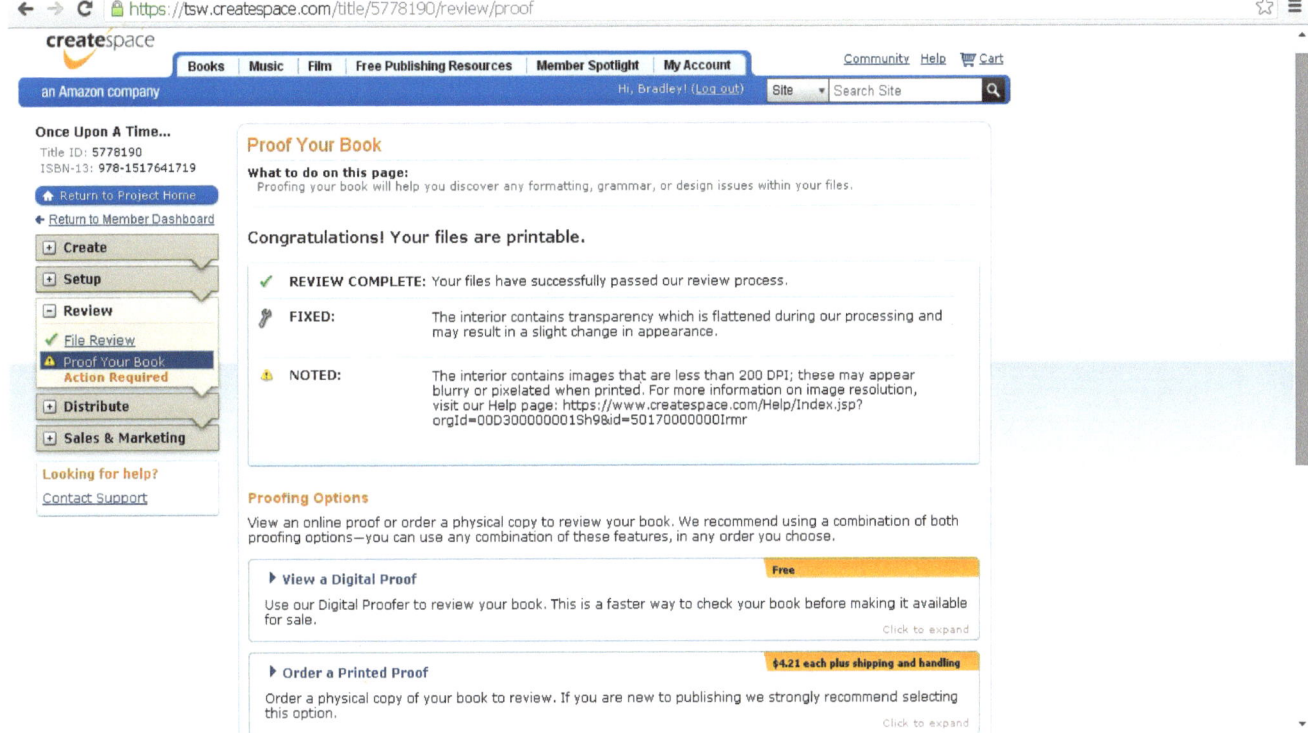

Proof Your Book Cont.

Issues that have been automatically fixed will be listed, as well as any printers notes.

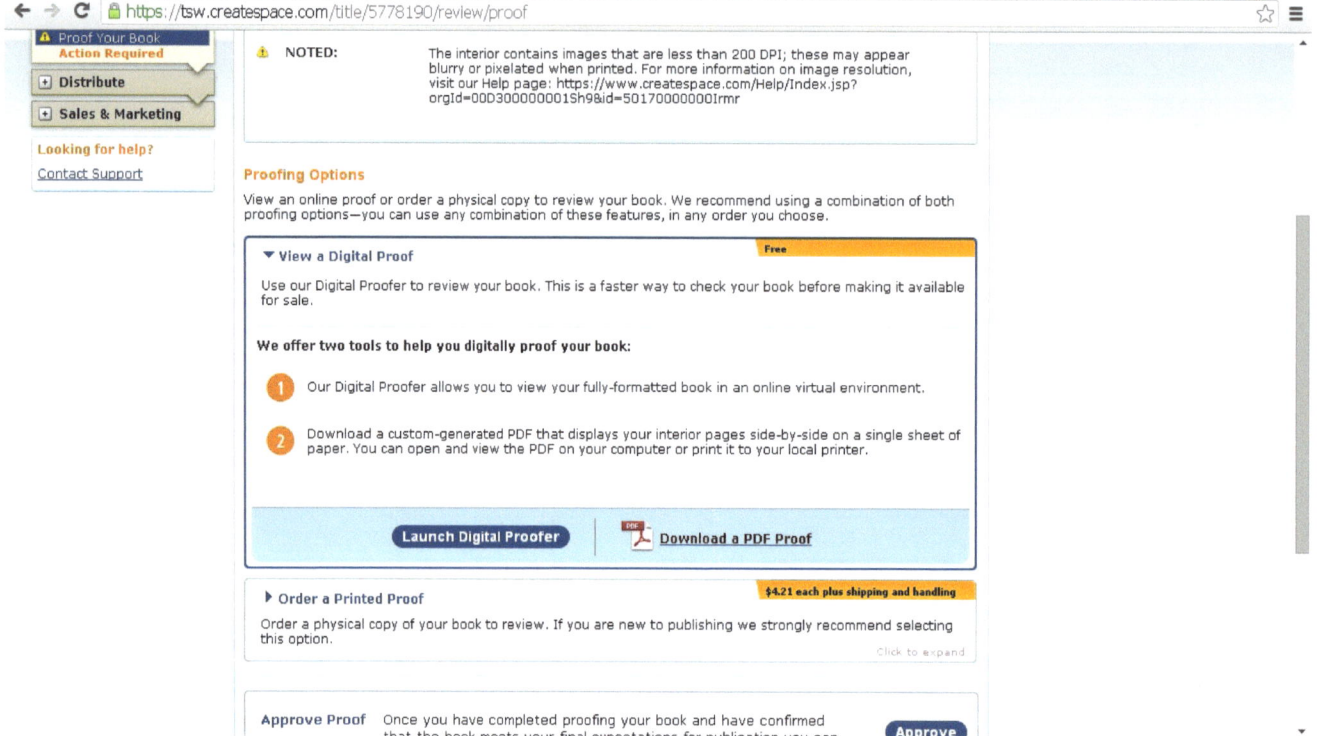

Free Digital Proof

You have 2 options for Proofing, View a Digital Proof of your book online (for Free), or order up to 5 Proof copies of your book. A printing and delivery fee will apply. For this book, I will explain the free digital proofing option.

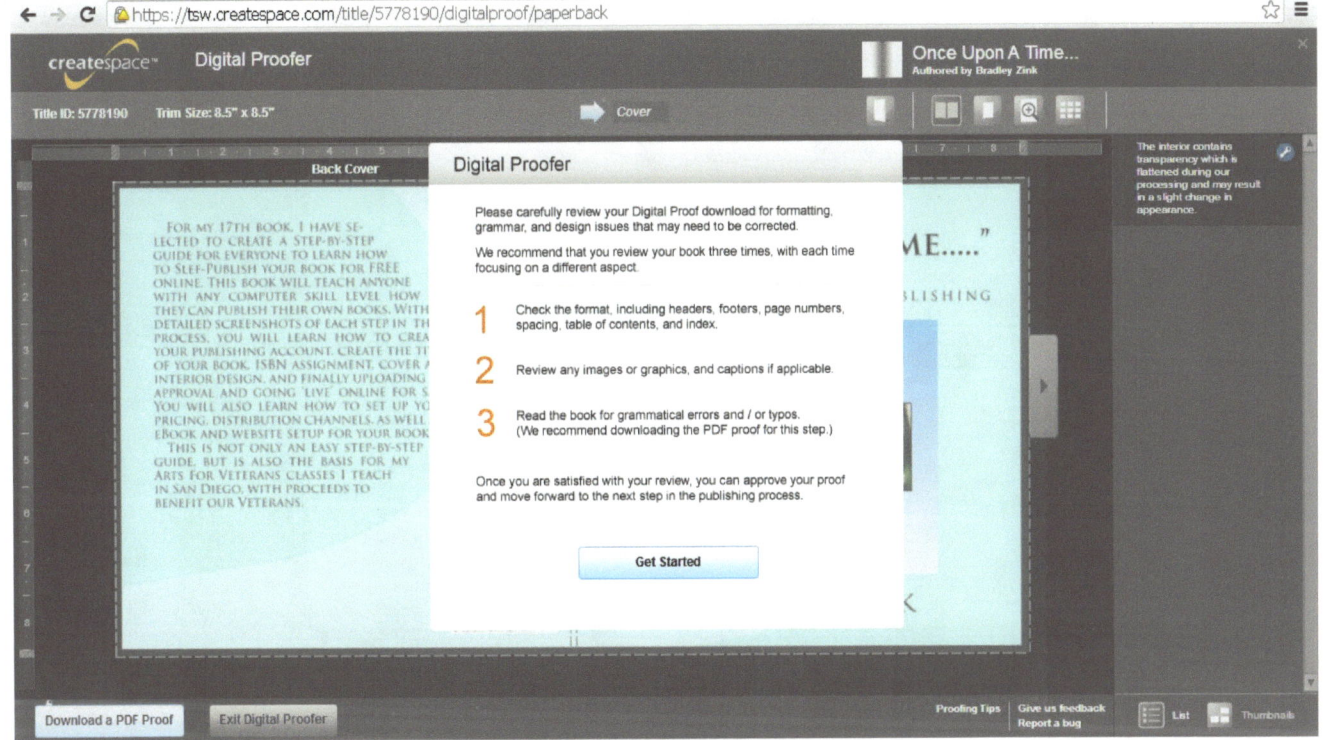

Digital Proofer

Similar to the File Review application, the Digital Proofer will show you exactly how your printed book will appear. Click Get started to continue the proofing process.

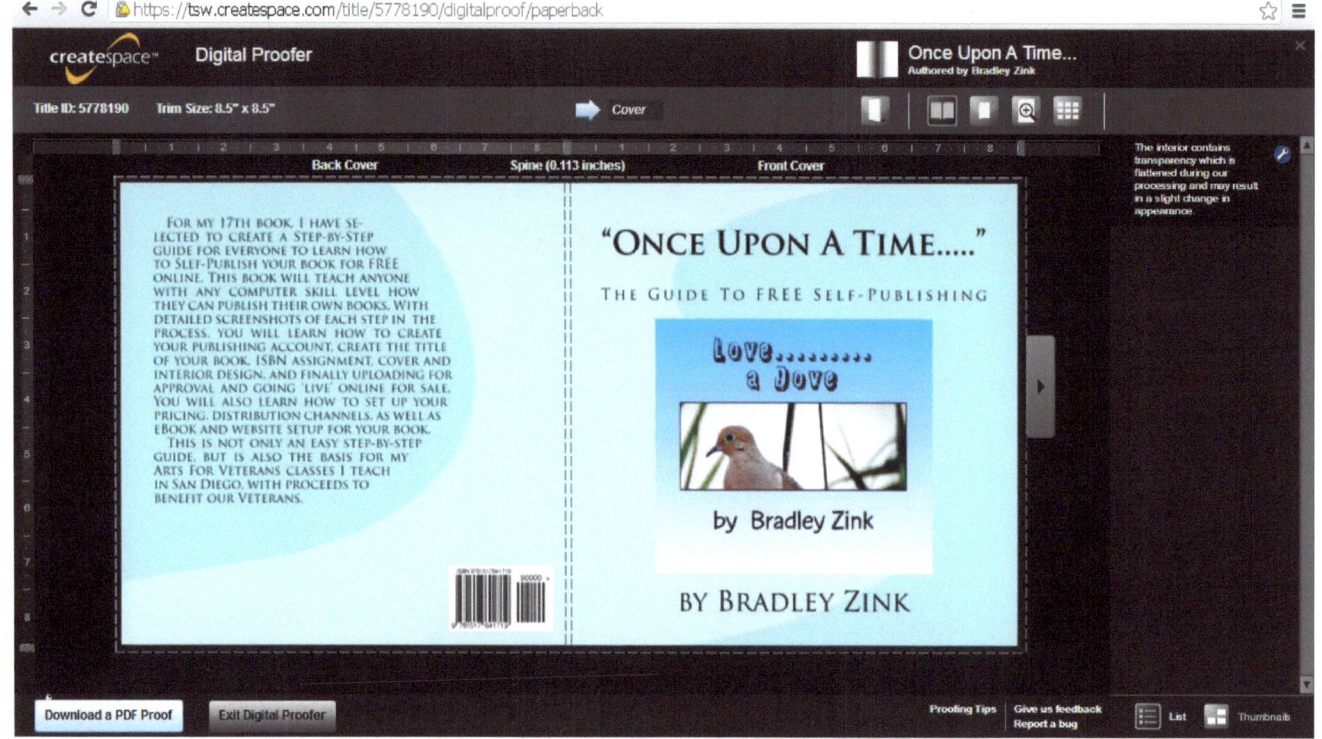

Digital Proofer Cont.

Cover to cover, the Digital Proofer is a very thorough tool for proofing your book.

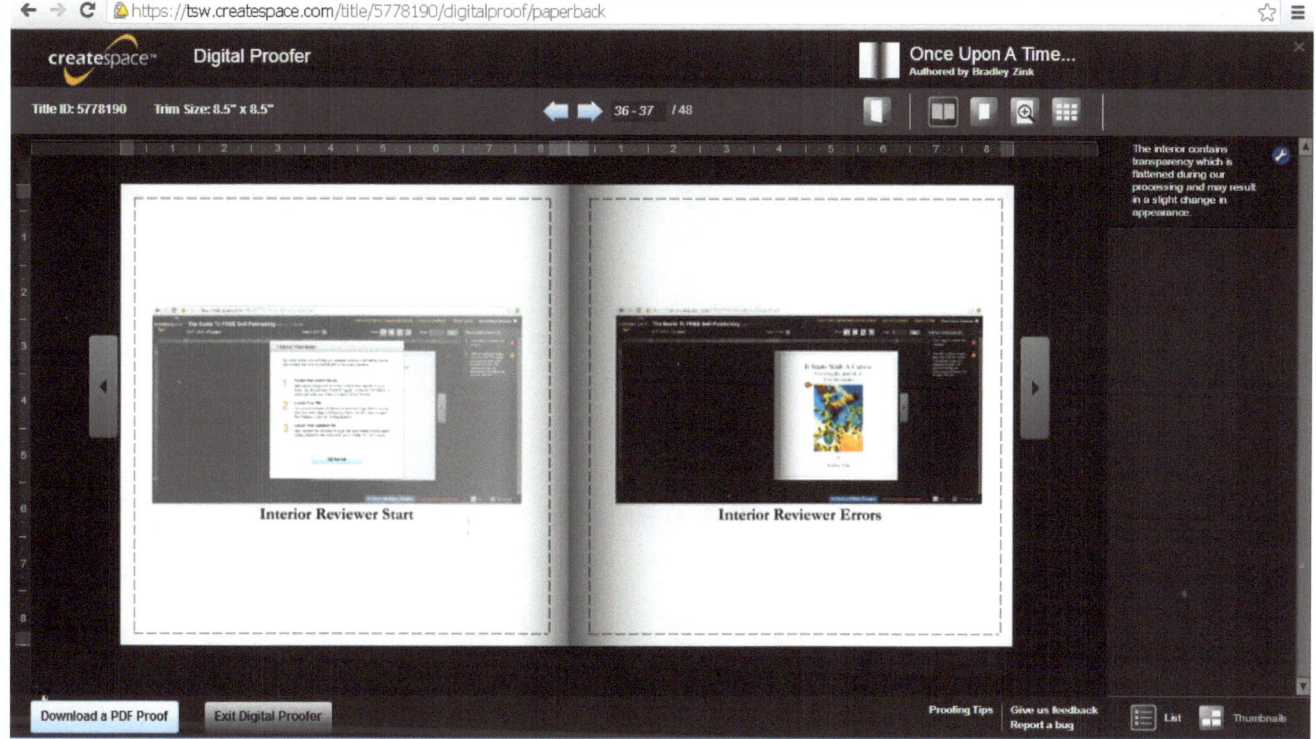

Digital Proofer Cont.

Be sure to check over every page, for this is what will be printed in the actual book.

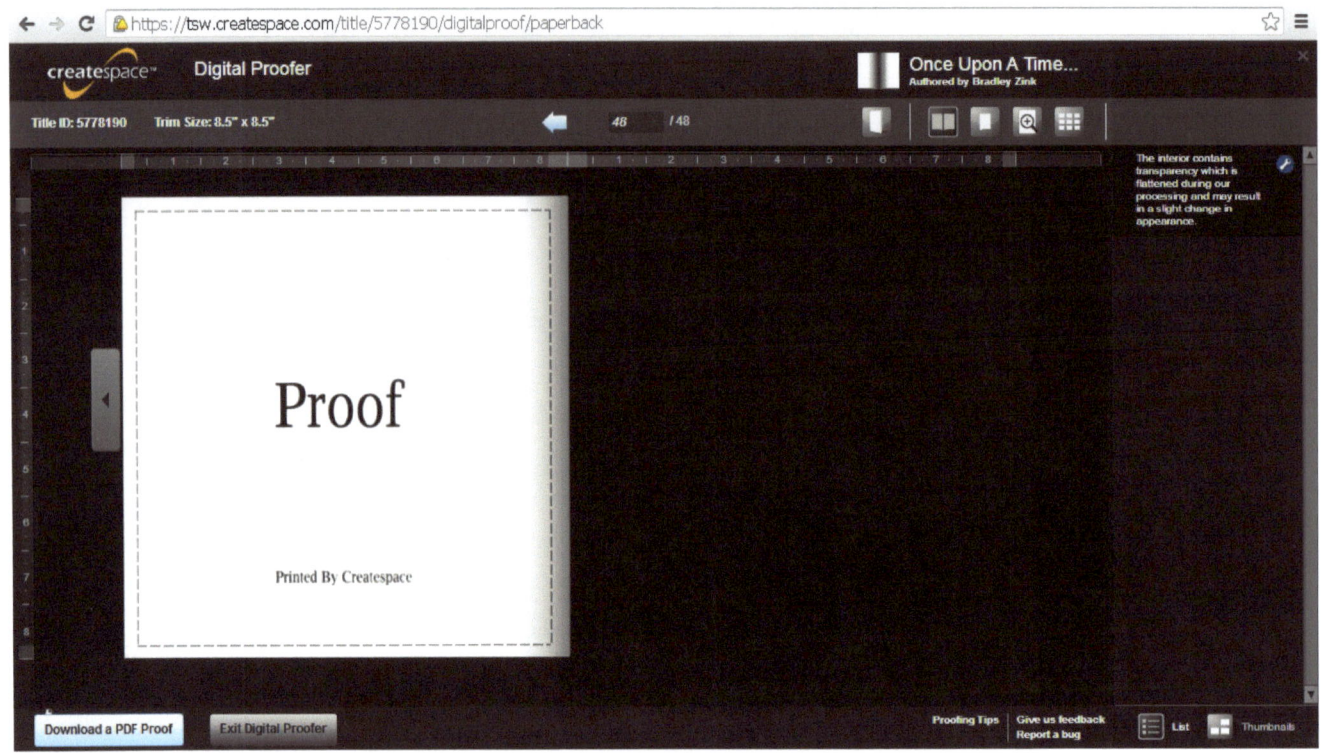

Digital Proofer Cont.

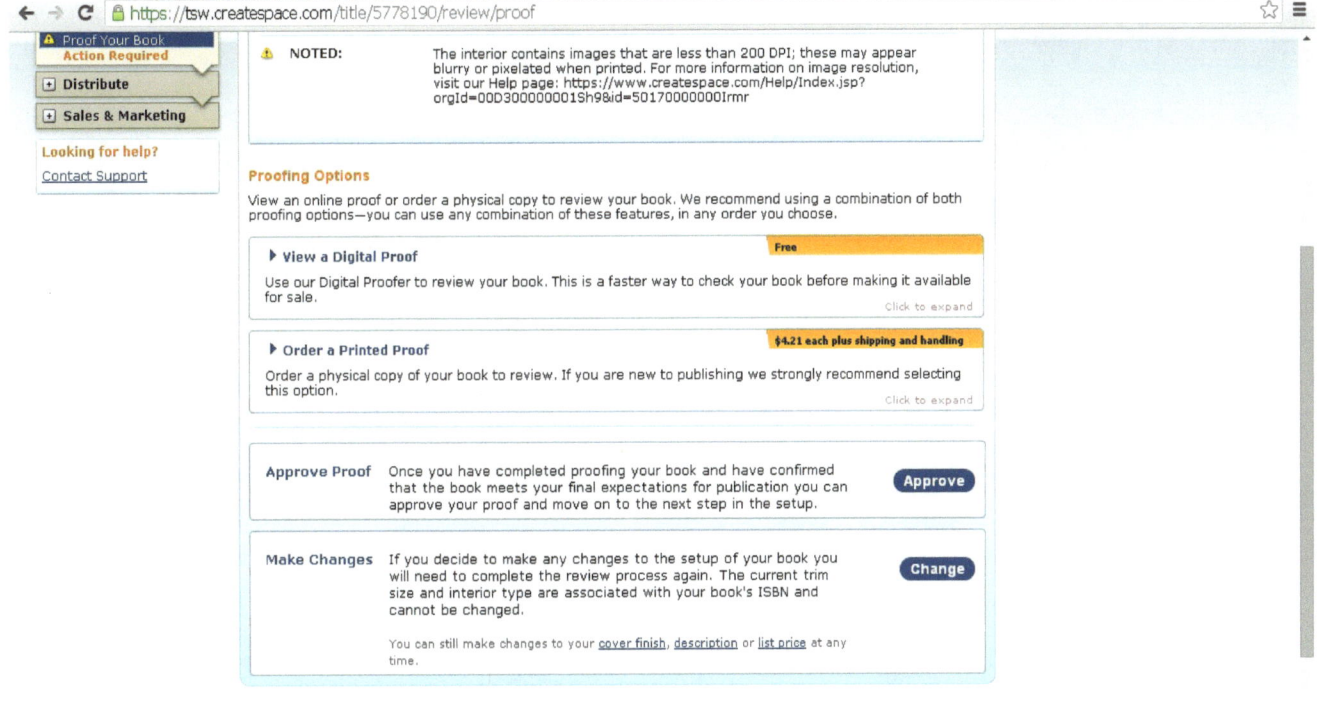

Approve or Change

If you detected any errors, go back through the process after making corrections in your Word file. If the book is ready for publishing, simply select Approve Proof.

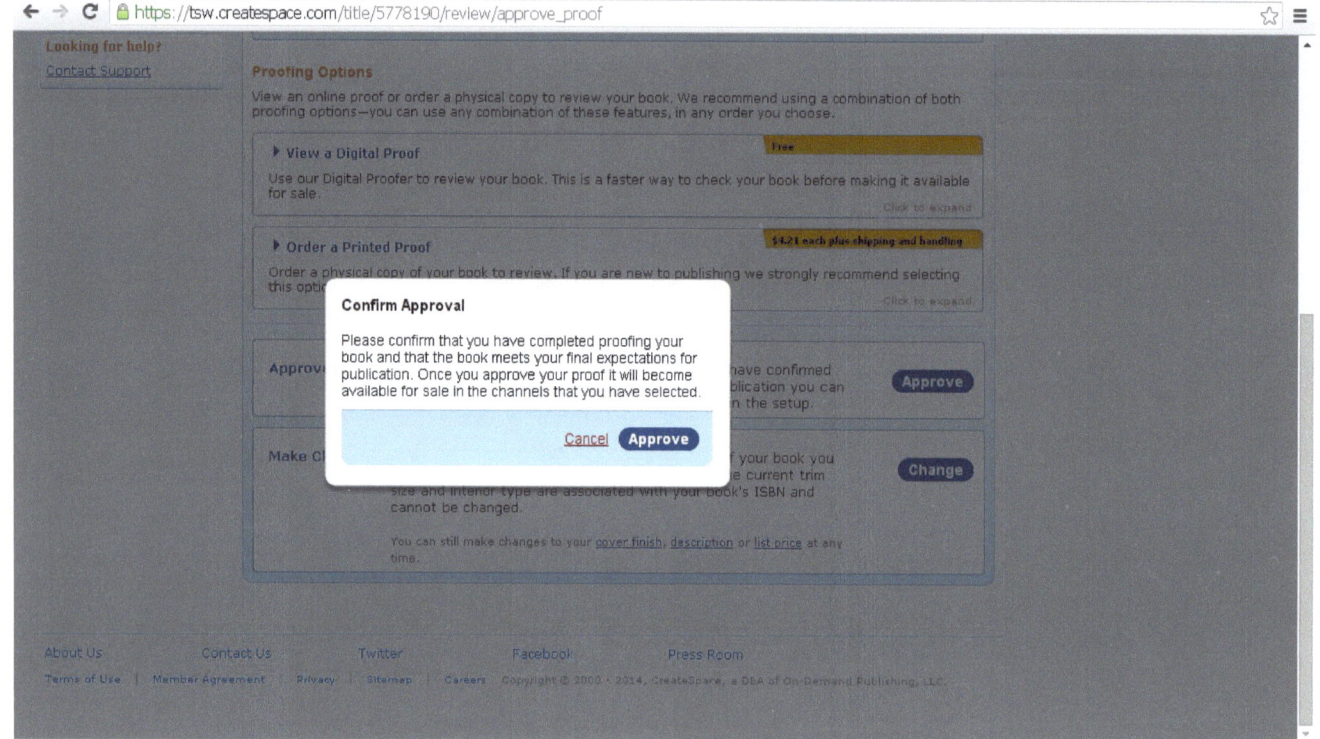

Confirm Approval

Confirm that you approve the Proof of your book.

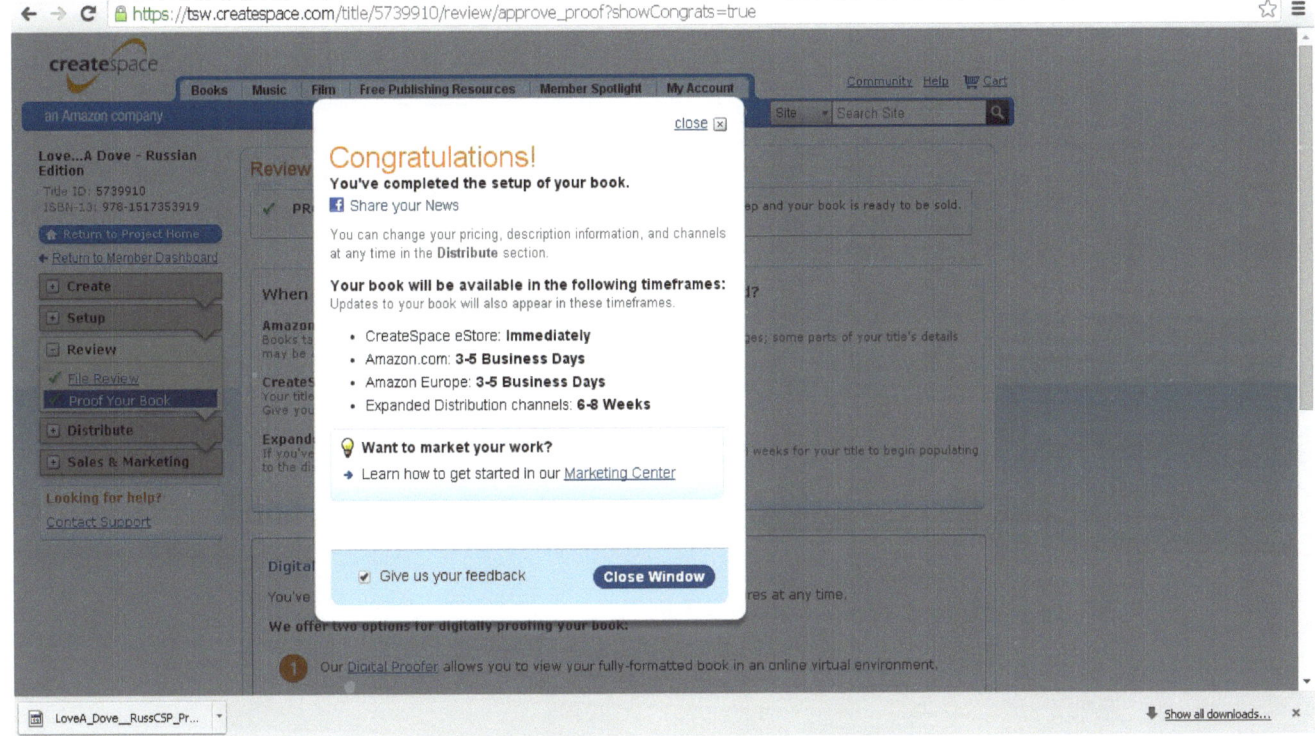

Approval Complete

Congratulations! You have just completed the process to publishing a book for FREE online. Now, share on your websites, social media pages and with the world. You are now a published author.

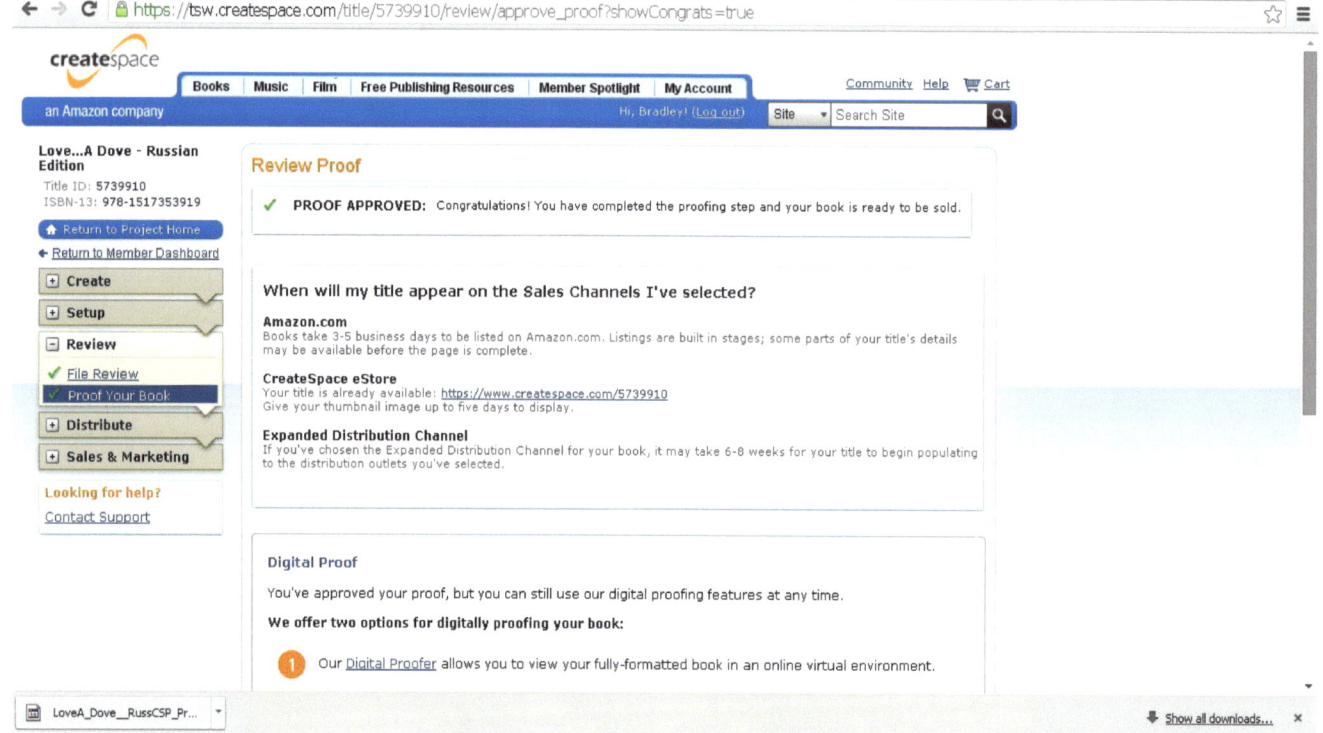

Proof Approved

Now that you have approved your proof and your book is live online, you can direct readers to your dedicated webpage for the book. Amazon will list after about 3-5 days, and Expanded Distribution Channels lists in about 6-8 weeks.

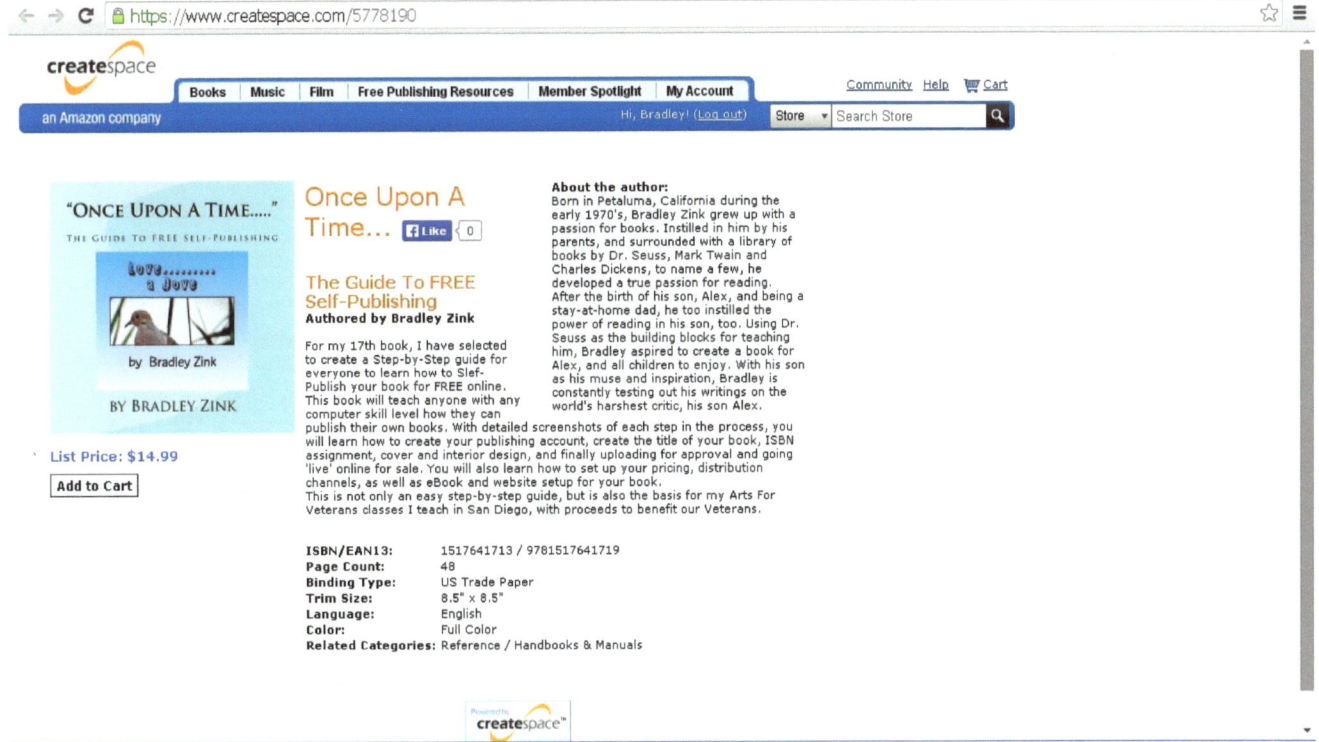

Book Live Online

Now your book is officially live online. It is available for purchase, with orders filled by Amazon.

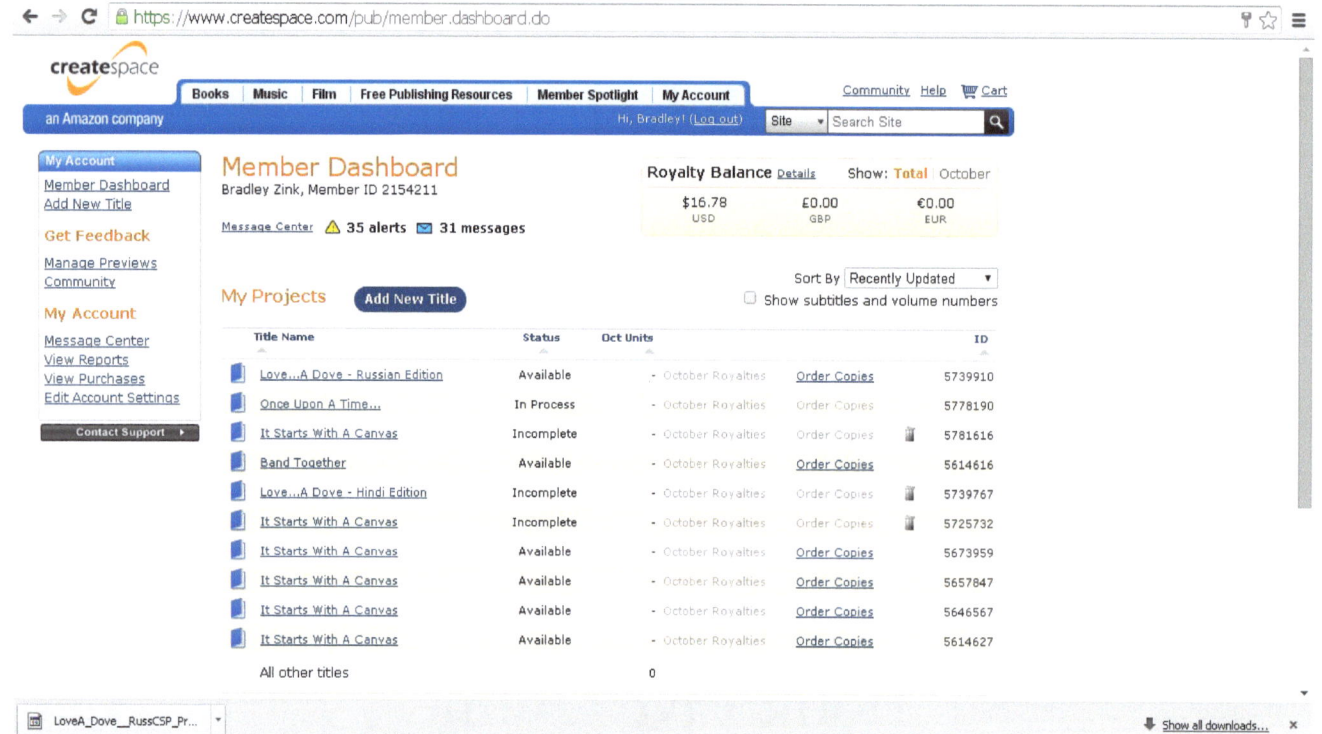

Available Status

Once you've approved the proof for your book, you will see that the Status has now changed to Available.

As you can see, the process of publishing online is rather straight-forward and streamlined to give you the best opportunity to produce a book without the expense of having a publisher. I hope this helps everyone who has ever dreamed about publishing their own book, and inspires others to accomplish the feat of Publishing your own Book!

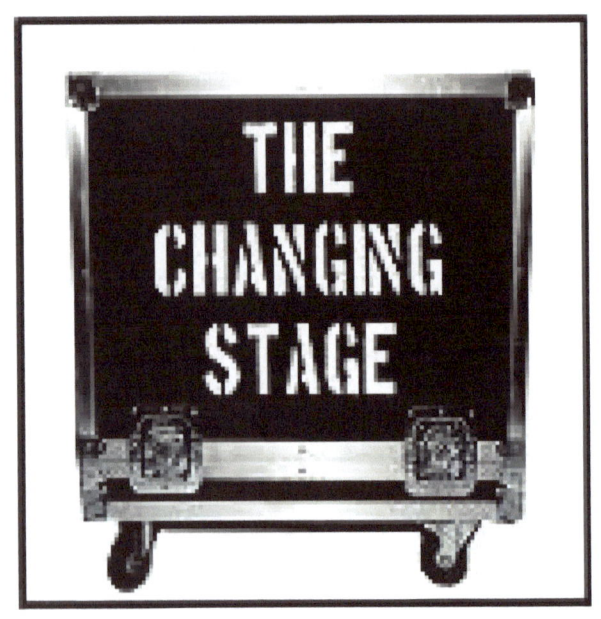

Traci B. Smith

TBS

Photography

Special

Thanks to my

Community Sponsors

RADIO BANDIEGO
Your Bands Revealed

ABOUT THE AUTHOR

Born in Petaluma, California during the early 1970's, Bradley Zink grew up with a passion for books. Instilled in him by his parents, and surrounded with a library of books by Dr. Seuss, Mark Twain and Charles Dickens, to name a few, he developed a true passion for reading. After the birth of his son, Alex, and being a stay-at-home dad, he too instilled the power of reading in his son, too. Using Dr. Seuss as the building blocks for teaching him, Bradley aspired to create a book for Alex, and all children to enjoy. With his son as his muse and inspiration, Bradley is constantly testing out his writings on the world's harshest critic, his son Alex.

www.ingramcontent.com/pod-product-compliance
Lightning Source LLC
Chambersburg PA
CBHW041458280526
45792CB00004B/1054